364.154   Smart, Ed.
SMA
          Bringing Elizabeth
          home.

$22.95

DATE			

Bringing *Elizabeth* Home

BRINGING
Elizabeth HOME

A Journey of Faith and Hope

ED AND LOIS SMART *with Laura Morton*

DOUBLEDAY

New York   London   Toronto   Sydney   Auckland

PUBLISHED BY DOUBLEDAY
a division of Random House, Inc.

DOUBLEDAY and the portrayal of an anchor with a dolphin
are registered trademarks of Random House, Inc.

Family photo of the Smarts, Christmas 2002, courtesy of Joy
Gough/ZUMA Press.

Photos of the Smarts at the White House courtesy of Robert
Bird/National Center for Missing & Exploited Children.

Book design by Erin L. Matherne and Tina Thompson

Cataloging-in-Publication Data is on file with the
Library of Congress.

ISBN 0-385-51214-7

PRINTED IN THE UNITED STATES OF AMERICA

[November 2003]

FIRST EDITION

4   5   6   7   8   9   10

This book is dedicated with love and gratitude

to our family—the Francoms and the Smarts.

And to our six wonderful beautiful children,

Charles, Elizabeth, Andrew, Mary Katherine, Edward, and William.

To all those who helped, prayed, and searched.

And to our Heavenly Father.

BRINGING *Elizabeth* HOME

Chapter 1

June 5, 2002, 3:58 a.m.

WE AWOKE TO THE SOUND of a voice filled with fright—that of our nine-year-old daughter, Mary Katherine.

"She's gone. Elizabeth is gone."

Mary Katherine stood by Lois's side of the bed, her head covered by her baby blanket. It wasn't unusual to have one of our children come into our room in the middle of the night, and at first we were certain it had just been a bad dream. Mary Katherine and Elizabeth shared a room, and sometimes Elizabeth would sleep in another room, especially if Mary Katherine had kicked her one too many times in her sleep.

She went on, "You won't find her. A man came and took her. He had a gun."

At the mention of a gun, it was obvious that something really out of the ordinary was going on, and Ed nervously sprang from bed to check every room in the house. Lois, panic rising, ran from the room and down the stairs, flicking every light switch on the wall, illuminating the kitchen and adjacent family room. We expected Elizabeth to pop up from the sofa, where she sometimes retreated. There was no motion. No child fast asleep. No sleepy-eyed angel asking, "What's going on?" Lois's eyes fell on the cut screen in the kitchen window, and she screamed in utter disbelief and shock. That's when we both realized that Mary Katherine's words had quickly become our worst nightmare.

Our daughter Elizabeth was gone.

Chapter 2

Although there are many things about this life that I do not understand,
there are some truths about which I no longer have any doubt.

—SHERI DEW

$\mathcal{E}$LIZABETH SMART is our daughter. When she was kidnapped, she became everyone's daughter. She belonged to America. We are not sure why the media picked up on Elizabeth's story, but people became aware of her abduction all around the world. Maybe it was because the media felt an affinity to Salt Lake City, having just been there for three weeks during the 2002 Winter Olympics. We may never know the reason. What separates one missing child from another? Is it race? Money? A slow news time? A holiday?

This has been a strange, hard, sometimes rewarding, but mostly painful journey. We didn't expect to be in the situation we awoke to the morning of June 5, 2002. We never dreamed we'd someday have to face the harrowing tragedy of losing our daughter at the hands of a stranger. We've all read stories about missing children, and surely our hearts go out to those families who endure the pain of losing a child. The odds are so against bringing a child home safely when they go missing. Ninety-eight percent of abducted children do not survive beyond the first thirty days.

How many times have you seen the face of a child on a "missing person" poster, or on a flyer in the mail with your discount coupons, or on the side of a milk carton, a billboard, or the evening news? Like most people, we always glanced, but we never really bothered to take a good long look at those faces, study their features, or ask ourselves if we had possibly seen this missing child. We hear about it all the time, but we think, "It'll never happen to me." But it can happen to you, because it happened to us. When we see those pictures now, we can't help but look at them and know the horror the parents are feeling. We truly know what they are going through.

We're the parents of six beautiful and amazing children, four boys and two girls, ranging from ages five to seventeen. Charles, our oldest son, is an avid soccer player who is now focused on mountain biking and downhill skiing. He's a senior in high school, and if you looked at his picture you'd probably correctly guess that he has a very active social life. Elizabeth, the next oldest, is a sophomore in high school this year. Andrew, who's in the eighth grade, is the practical joker in our family. He is a whiz with electronics, and we depend on him as the only person in our home who knows how to operate the audiovisual equipment. Andrew loves to snowmobile, so once as an incentive to help him take an interest in school we offered to upgrade our family snowmobile if he put in more time studying. It was the first time Andrew ever brought home straight A's. He even started reading the newspaper in addition to his schoolwork, although he was mostly just looking for that new snowmobile in the classifieds! Andrew also has a knack for playing the banjo. People have stopped us and said that Mary Katherine looks like a budding Grace Kelly. She's very artistic, both visually and musically. She loves playing her harp, painting and drawing horses, dogs, and fairies, and making clay animals, and she is currently taking a watercolor class that she very much enjoys. Her dog, Ollie, is her pride and joy. If teaching the harp doesn't work out for her, she could definitely be a veterinarian. Edward has presence—everyone knows when he is in the room. He is extremely inquisitive and seems to know everything. Even if he doesn't know the answer to a question, he'll make something up, and it always sounds viable. He became convinced that our new black Labrador, Siah, is part German shepherd because Siah is always on the lookout, and he heard that German shepherds are great watch-dogs. Edward plays the piano and loves to ride his bike. He is the only one of our children who loves to snowboard. William is our baby. He is a sweet boy who loves his brothers and sisters. He's beginning to branch out and discover his interests, such as baking cookies, cutting out paper objects, and blowing big bubbles with his gum. He is also a terrific little skier. He never wants to be left out, and he needs to always be where the action is.

Our extended combined family of the Smarts (Ed's family) and Francoms (Lois's family) reaches nearly triple digits, making holidays, birthdays, and graduations rather lively and frequent events. When Elizabeth disappeared, we were so fortunate to have such a large family to depend and lean on. The Francom family and the Smart family equally supported us, offering unflinching and constant encouragement throughout the nine months Elizabeth was gone and in the months since she has been home. We are forever grateful for the love and backing of our family and friends and so many others whom we don't know but were there during our time of need.

This book is an opening of our pained hearts. Every parent, at one time or another, has surely thought about the unspeakable, unthinkable question: "What would you do if one of your children was taken from you?" It is a terrifying prospect, one we sincerely hope you will never have to face. It was by far the worst nightmare we, as a family, as a couple, and as parents could have ever imagined. The intrusion on our family extended far beyond the empty seat at the dinner table or the gaping hole in our hearts. All of our five other children felt the impact of their sister's disappearance. In many ways, when Elizabeth was taken, all of our children were taken.

Having given a great deal of thought to writing this book, we knew in our hearts that our journey is one that had to be shared because it is more than the story of our daughter's kidnapping—it is a story of great hope, strong faith, and our trust in our Heavenly Father. As a family, we are practicing members of the Church of Jesus Christ of Latter-Day Saints, also known as Mormons. Our beliefs played a huge part in getting us through our crisis, but they weren't something we turned to as a result of that crisis. We have always been devout people of faith and active members of our church. Though our experience was terribly painful, through our faith and a trust in God's power we gained tremendous strength, which became the cornerstone of how we survived. Having our daughter back home, in our arms, is nothing short of a miracle. It is the ultimate proof that God answers prayers. Granted, sometimes the answer is not the one we pray for, but still, it remains an answer. We feel truly blessed that He answered our prayers the way we had hoped for, though we realize, regretfully, that is not always the outcome in kidnapping cases. We have met so many families with missing children, and we've seen how deep their pain goes. It is something you never get over. In an instant, life as you know it is changed. Not knowing Elizabeth's whereabouts was terribly painful. There were so many days we simply could not accept why someone would do something like this. We can only imagine what it is like for those families who never see their children again or hear the news that their child has been found dead. We dreaded every phone call, every knock on the door, and every time we were asked to "come down to the station" for fear we, too, would hear the unthinkable news.

What we hope to convey through our journey of faith and hope is that with a strong belief in God and His power, all things are possible. *Miracles do happen.*

Former church president and prophet Spencer W. Kimball, author of *Faith Precedes the Miracle,* wrote many passages in his book that touched us and helped us understand how to better handle adversity. He wrote that in life "there are reservoirs of many kinds. Some reservoirs are to store water. Some are to store food. There should also be reservoirs of knowledge to meet future needs; reservoirs of courage to overcome the floods of fear that put uncertainty in lives; reservoirs of stamina; and reservoirs of faith—especially reservoirs of faith—so that when the world presses upon us, we stand firm and strong; when the temptations of a decaying world about us draw on our energies, sap our spiritual vitality, and seek to pull us down, we need a storage of faith that can carry us over the dull, difficult, terrifying moments, disappointments, disillusionments and adversity, want, confusion, and frustration." We'd like to think that we discovered reservoirs of all kinds while Elizabeth was missing. We tapped our resources, both internal and external, to chart our course through this nine-month nightmare.

Since Elizabeth returned home, there have been many questions surrounding what happened to her while she was gone. As her parents, we wish to protect our daughter's privacy and will not share the terrifying details of her captivity. We feel privacy is something Elizabeth, having survived nine months of torment, is entitled to. Perhaps someday she will choose to publicly share her story. That is *her* decision to make—not ours. We are just overwhelmed to have her home, where she belongs, well on her way to recovering and getting back to being a normal teenager.

We will never be able to get those nine months back, and for that we feel robbed. Birthdays came and went. Vacations came and went. A school year passed by. We tried to live as normally as we could, but when Elizabeth was taken from us, our definition of normal changed. Given the sudden thrust into the media spotlight and the almost unbearable pain every night when we tucked our children into bed, we did the best we could. We are not perfect, but until the morning of June 5, our lives felt blessed in every way. With her disappearance, we had to reevaluate our priorities—not that they were so far out of line to begin with. Like most people, when life is sailing along as ours had been, we simply took for granted the family we had built together. Ed focused on work and Lois focused on being a stay-at-home mom. We both thought life was as close to perfect as it could get. But losing Elizabeth brought one point painfully home: *Nothing* is more important in this world than our family. Not money. Not work. Not a fancy new car or an expensive big house. Family, the prayers of so many friends and strangers, and our trust in God are what got us through this experience—and having survived, we have no doubt that we will persevere in any situation as long as we have those three things in our life.

We recognize that when we decided to utilize the media in our search for Elizabeth, we automatically gave up control over our story. It was a trade-off—one that we understand. We never wanted to be in the public eye. We would have been very content to have led the rest of our lives having never given a media update, an interview, or a public plea for the safe return of our daughter. But that isn't how things worked out. Elizabeth was kidnapped. As parents, we would have done anything for her safe return. Aside from God's help, the media was the most important instrument in bringing our daughter home. We were able to keep Elizabeth's name, photo, and story alive even when all the evidence pointed in a darker direction. Though our story is filled with many incredible twists and turns, we never lost focus on what was important: bringing Elizabeth home.

Once Elizabeth was found, we believed—however naively— that was the end of the story. There was no way to effectively turn off the media spotlight we had been under for nine months. Elizabeth has a long, bright future, and we want to protect her in as many ways as we can so that she can have a "normal" life. There have been so many outrageous, hurtful, and salacious stories about what really happened with respect to the kidnapping and the investigation, and now that Elizabeth is home we simply cannot allow those stories to stand. We are telling the story from our perspective so that, at the very least, we as a family gain some control over the information and misinformation that has been circulating now for well over a year. This book is a true account of what we endured in the nine months that Elizabeth was missing. Others may choose to tell a different version of what happened during those nine months, and there is very little we can do to stop those efforts. What we can do is speak our truth. We cooperated in the production of the CBS movie that tells a shortened and modified version of Elizabeth's story, but this book contains the genuine facts of what actually happened.

Every one of us has the ability to make choices in life, but in making those choices we also have to live by them. When a story goes public, there is very little anyone can do to control the way that story is told or the opinions that are formulated as a result of media attention, especially when that attention reaches massive proportions, as it did in our case. We are so grateful for the help we received from all of our friends in the media, especially those who supported our search in every possible way. By writing this book, we risk the chance that our integrity may be challenged. It wouldn't be the first time. We endured that kind of public scrutiny the first few months Elizabeth was gone. When you lose a child the way we did, your honesty and integrity are the first things people question. There were so many unsubstantiated rumors about our family, our daughter, and the abduction. We lived through all of them. But in view of the situation, we feel that Elizabeth should not have to suffer one more minute of pain from her ordeal, nor should her own honesty and integrity ever be challenged.

Our decision to write this book was made as a family—to ensure that the story be told the right way, with tremendous appreciation for all of those who kept Elizabeth in their prayers, deep gratitude to those who volunteered their time to help us search for our daughter, and humble admiration for the investigators, police officers, detectives, and FBI agents who kept the search going until Elizabeth was found. But the main reason we wrote this book was to give infinite thanks to our Heavenly Father for answering our prayers.

Chapter 3

Prayer is not asking. Prayer is putting oneself in the hands of God, at His disposition, and listening to His voice in the depth of our hearts.

—MOTHER TERESA

WE BELIEVE THE LORD hears everyone's prayers. There are good, decent people from all walks of life, in all religions, with many different beliefs. We don't feel that the Lord answered our prayers because we are special, righteous, chosen, or because we are members of the Church of Jesus Christ of Latter-Day Saints. There are good people and not so good people in every religion and in all walks of life. Brian David Mitchell had been a member of the church but was excommunicated because his beliefs became radical and self-serving.

He had been slowly digressing for years. We have all made our share of mistakes and will probably continue to, but along the way, we'd like to believe that we are improving as people, as husband and wife, as parents, friends, and community leaders. Our parents raised us to believe in God, to have faith, and to rely on the word of the Lord. We have raised our children the same way, and we hope and pray that our legacy continues when we have grandchildren and great-grandchildren. All we can hope for is that we have done what is right as parents and role models for our children. When you're young, you rely on the adults in your life to lead by example. At some point, it is hoped, you discover what you think and believe on your own. That's how you go forward in life.

Faith ebbs and flows. There were many times after Elizabeth disappeared when we both felt our faith was being tested. We questioned the greater meaning of why we were faced with this extreme adversity. It forced us to face our weaknesses, our inadequacies, and every time we felt low, we both wondered how Elizabeth was coping. We never let our minds wander to those dark thoughts for long. We wanted to believe that Elizabeth was being protected and watched over, that she was being helped. That was the motivation to pull ourselves up by our bootstraps and face the next day. We had no choice. We had to be there, together, strong, and prepared—just in case this was the day Elizabeth came home. In the long run, it strengthened our faith and made us aware of our weaknesses and shortcomings. There were so many times in prayer when we felt as if we were pleading for life—for Elizabeth's life, our lives, and the life of everyone around us. We asked our Heavenly Father for forgiveness and for the strength to go on. We humbly asked for the courage to face the days when we had no answers.

The story of Elizabeth's kidnapping has been a mystery—complete with suspects, detectives, and a surprise ending—and even now it is still unfolding. It is a dark, disturbing tale. It is a journey of hope and faith, an odyssey filled with good and evil, shadow and light. It is a story we hope people will still be talking about one hundred years from now—not because it is about our daughter, but because it is a story about all of us. It is a remarkable saga of a community and a country banding together in collective prayer and coming together with a common goal: to bring Elizabeth home.

So many people shared their thoughts and prayers with our family when Elizabeth was kidnapped. It came to feel as if the entire world was praying for our daughter. We received tens of thousands of letters from people who said this story impacted their lives. Perhaps our mission is to help bring people closer to one another—and closer to God—through the telling of our experience. The letters we received during the nine months gave us strength and helped us remember that we had the faith of all of you to carry us through. These letters were amazing. They began arriving from people all over the world before we had any idea that our story was global. The unified sentiment was to "keep the faith." And we did. Thank you to all of you who took the time to write to us and share your thoughts, feelings, and heartfelt prayers. Your letters were truly a priceless gift to us.

There is nothing as pure as the faith of a child. Among these many thousands of letters, incredibly it was the letters we received from children that most reminded us not to give up hope. Children have an unbelievable gift. Their thoughts are so honest and untainted. Of course Elizabeth would come home, they felt. It was their expectation. One of our young nieces said to us, "They stole her body but not her soul." How profound and true. It filled our hearts to read those letters and be reminded of the beautiful simplicity of that pure faith.

We've had to make numerous difficult decisions in our lives, but none as hard as the ones we've made over the past year and a half. To understand our choices, we feel it is important that you know how we came to make them. We are deeply religious people. We have raised our children to believe in the same core beliefs that we both grew up with. It is relevant and essential to learn some of the foundations of our religious beliefs so that our story transcends the boundaries of religion and stretches into what became a stronger belief in a higher being and a better understanding of our faith. To us, the best and most effective way to share our beliefs is to live them.

As with all religions, there are certain basic tenets that constitute the core of our faith, the Church of Jesus Christ of Latter-Day Saints. Our faith is founded on a belief in God—that we are all His children and that He is always there for us. Beyond the basic doctrines of the church, we often create our own individual codes of conduct based on what brings us, as individuals, closer to God. As church members we are taught to study things in our own minds and to rely on personal revelation. We are given commandments and basic guidelines of conduct by the Lord, but the details of how we interpret and carry out those principles are between us, our families, and the Lord. As Latter-Day Saints, we have a language that is specific to our beliefs, so throughout this book, some of the terms we refer to may not be immediately familiar. We will make a point to explain those terms so that you'll know what we're talking about. For example, we refer to our home church congregation as a "ward." Wards are groups of members who are led by a bishop, his two counselors, and other ward leaders. It's a lay ministry. Each ward is given a name that is unique to its area. The ward that we attend is the Arlington Hills ward. Its members make up our ward family. While Elizabeth was missing, members from our ward and other wards from all over Utah and surrounding states came out in strong support to help our search effort.

Our community in Salt Lake City is made up of faithful people—faithful people of all religious backgrounds, not just Mormons. We were amazed by how quickly our community, and so many others, stepped up to help with our search efforts, donating food, water, tents, flashlights—and most of all, their time. In addition, many organizations and clubs allowed us use of their planes, helicopters, search dogs, and horses in our search. We marveled at how everyone came out to show support and lend a helping hand. Our oldest son, Charles, often pointed out that people he would have never expected to see were turning up day after day to help look for his sister. We had always thought of ourselves as little pebbles in a huge lake. We thought that nobody really knew us and that we were just an average family leading an average life. The first day we searched for Elizabeth, more than a thousand people turned out to help us look. By the following Monday, there were over eight thousand searchers! There couldn't have been more love anywhere in the world that day than there was in Salt Lake City.

The mission of the Church of Jesus Christ of Latter-Day Saints is to "invite all to come unto Christ" (D&C 20:59) "and be perfected in him" (Moroni 10:32). We study scripture from the Bible, including the Old Testament and the New Testament, as well as the Book of Mormon and other scriptures, which represent the continuing of Revelation. The Book of Mormon is a companion volume and a second witness of Christ.

Pray in your families unto the Father, always in my name
that your wives and your children may be blessed.
—3 NEPHI 18:21

Our beliefs place a tremendous emphasis on families and family life. The first commandment that God gave to Adam and Eve pertained to their potential for parenthood as husband and wife. Husbands and wives have a solemn responsibility to love and care for each other and for their children. As parents, we have been taught to raise our children in love and righteousness and to teach them to love and serve one another. Happiness in our family is achieved through the teachings of the Lord Jesus Christ. It is achieved and maintained on the principles of faith, prayer, repentance, forgiveness, respect, love, compassion, and work.

To have a family member go missing was excruciating for us, as it has been for so many other parents. Because we believe that marriages and families have an eternal bond, extending beyond death, we are considered to be a family for all of eternity. Husbands and wives who marry in the Temple are sealed together. Children who are born to parents who have been married in the Temple are likewise considered to be part of the eternal family unit. We make a special point of sharing this with you because it played a big part in helping us, as Elizabeth's family, cope with her disappearance. The belief in an eternal family gave us great hope that we would one day be reunited with our daughter—whether here on earth or in the hereafter.

Ye are commanded in all things to ask of God, who giveth liberally.
—D&C 46:7

We know that to some of you the ideas and principles associated with being members of our church may seem unusual—maybe even hard to understand. For us, they are a way of life. We have lived as members of our church our whole lives, and we are grateful for our heritage, beliefs, and relationship with God. Ours is a religion that emphasizes freedom of choice. We are not perfect people. We are two humans who continue to grow on a daily basis, making choices along the way that we can live by.

Did we ever ask why this was happening to us? All the time. We had many more questions than answers. We're not sure that we expected an actual answer to "why" Elizabeth was taken from us, but through those kinds of questions we were summoning spiritual strength and pleading for the power to endure. Enduring, on some levels, meant that we had to accept that the situation was out of our hands. We were doing everything we could to bring Elizabeth home. Scriptures teach us that there are many things we can do to improve the line of communication between ourselves and the Lord. These include fasting and praying. Fasting is a practice whereby your spirit becomes more in tune with God. It's a form of self-discipline. Your spirit is in control, not your body. Your body needs food for nourishment. Your spirit needs a different kind of nourishment gained through a strong relationship with the Lord. Fasting invites the spirit of revelation. Through prayer and fasting, our faith was significantly strengthened, and we were more at peace knowing that this was bigger than we were and that it was in the Lord's hands and out of our control.

There are numerous passages in scripture that emphatically remind us there is indeed soul-strengthening power that comes from impassioned prayer. Our prayers were constant and ever-present. We often prayed that God would soften the hearts of Elizabeth's abductors. We prayed for Elizabeth's protection. We prayed for her safe return. We were not certain of God's plan for us or Elizabeth, but we knew that it was not God who took Elizabeth—so how could we place any blame on Him?

———

Free agency is the concept that individuals should be free to make decisions that affect their own lives, even if those decisions are wrong. Elizabeth's captors, Brian David Mitchell and Wanda Barzee, acted on their free agency the night Brian broke into our home and stole Elizabeth. Though they have the ability to freely choose their actions, they are not free from the consequences. Subsequently, neither are we—nor is Elizabeth. We are all accountable for our own actions, right and wrong.

We both are uncertain how we would have survived Elizabeth's abduction had it not been for our strong faith and beliefs. More important than that, we don't know how Elizabeth would have survived. We have raised her with the ability to think freely, make good choices, and to believe in a loving Heavenly Father. She is so strong, and we are extremely proud of her. We felt certain that Elizabeth had the inner strength to get through an ordeal such as hers. We knew, without a doubt, that her faith was unshakable. Like Job, she descended into hell and surfaced.

Chapter 4

Lois

For if there be no faith among the children of men
God can do no miracle among them . . .

—Ether 12:12

I come from a very large family, the second youngest with five brothers and three sisters. In my family there is a long tradition of strong women, women such as my grandmother, Genevieve Pettit, who grew up on a farm in Arizona. Even as a four-year-old child she had many responsibilities. Every morning she would go with her father to milk the cows, carrying tiny buckets to collect the stripping, which is what butter is made from. One morning when the cows had broken out of the corral, her father went ahead to collect and bring them back, leaving her to walk alone along the long path from the house to the corral. Her mother encouraged her to hurry but to stay on the path so as to not get lost. Along the way, Grandmother stopped abruptly when she saw a rattlesnake coiled up alongside the path. Before she could back away it attacked, biting her on the knee. When her mother saw her sit down on the ground, she realized something was wrong and raced out to help her. Back then a rattlesnake bite was invariably fatal. Her mother carried her to the yard and placed her in a hammock that hung between two large trees next to their home. Her leg turned black from the poison. When nearby Hopi Indians heard that a child had been bitten, they came to see her and offer remedies and gifts. The Indians were kind to the family, but they were also certain my grandmother was facing death. Her parents placed poultices on the wound and prayed over her knee, staying by her side through the day and night. The next morning, to everyone's surprise, the venom was oozing out of her knee. Grandmother was weak from the bite for months after, and couldn't walk for a while, but she lived and eventually was completely healed. She had a strong will to live, and this has been passed along to the women in my family for generations. Elizabeth is certainly no exception to this trait.

The Francom family has always been one of strong faith. From the time I was a child, and all throughout my life, I believe I have witnessed many miracles. Through scripture, the Lord makes it very clear that faith is not developed by miracles, but that miracles are a result of great faith. Miracles are around us every day, but we need to learn how to see them. In life, there are no coincidences. Things that seemingly happen "out of the blue" are never really just random. When I was a child, our family would take vacations that usually involved all eleven of us piling into the family station wagon. One time while driving to Lake Tahoe, we were running very low on gas and my father looked desperately for a gas station, but there was none to be found. My mother studied Dad's trusty map and thought she'd found a shortcut to the next town. Soon after taking this new route we realized it was not a shortcut at all, and we indeed ran out of gas at the top of a large hill. I remember my father saying a prayer and then letting the car coast down the hill. At the bottom of the hill, he steered the car around a bend in the road, and there we found a man sitting in his truck with a barrel tank of gas in the back, complete with a nozzle and hose. The man readily filled our tank, and when my father tried to pay he refused to accept even a dime. I have no idea what the driver was doing out there in the middle of nowhere, but there he was, just sitting at the bottom of that hill waiting for us. We marveled at the notion that God heard our prayer—and answered it with a tank of gas in the middle of nowhere.

When my younger brother was eighteen months old, he contracted meningitis and encephalitis. I was three years old at the time, but I can remember the profound effect it had on our family. We prayed for him constantly. Fearing the worst, the doctors had told my mother to go home and tend to her other children. They didn't think my brother was going to pull through, and if he did, he'd certainly live the rest of his life with physical challenges. Yet my mother wouldn't leave his side. She had eight other children to tend to, but she couldn't leave my brother alone to die. The faith she had was incredibly strong. She knew he'd be healed through the blessings he received—and in the end, he was. He is alive today and is a brilliant, successful married man and father who survived his illness with no side effects whatsoever. The family faith overpowered the medical prognosis. That, to me, was another miracle.

Because faith is so strong in my family, it was vitally important to me that I marry someone whose faith matched my own. I had serious doubts as to whether I would ever be able to find the right person, but when I met Ed, something just clicked. I was twenty-seven and he was twenty-nine. I had traveled a lot, and I was working and enjoying life. Ed was working in real estate, buying and selling properties. We both knew what we were looking for, and we found it in each other. There was no use in wasting any more time. We were engaged after twelve dates and married a month later, in December 1984.

Elizabeth has followed this example with a strong faith of her own. When she was eight years old, she was baptized as a member of the church. She had been taught that she could pray anytime, anywhere, and that a loving Heavenly Father would hear her prayers. At that time we took a weekend trip to Ed's parents' mountain cabin, located not too far from our home in Salt Lake City. It was springtime, and everything in the mountains was in full bloom. Elizabeth loves horses, and she was eager to go for a ride. It's often been said that she plays the harp like an angel and rides a horse like a cowboy. That completely captures the spirit and essence of our daughter.

Her grandpa enjoys taking all of the children riding. His favorite trail, called "The Salt Trail," winds its way up the mountain to a meadow, where the children could stop to let the horses graze and rest. Especially at that time of year, the view down at the canyon and meadows overflowing with blooming wildflowers is spectacular.

Elizabeth dismounted her horse but didn't have a tight hold on the reins. Her horse pulled the reins from her hands and bolted back down to the pasture, leaving Elizabeth standing horseless at the top of the trail. Grandpa often said that you can never let the horse think he's the boss, because if you do, it's hard to break him of that habit, so it was important to find the horse. Since it was spring, there was no trodden-down path for her to follow. Elizabeth got lost and couldn't find her way back, and she thought for certain she would be in big trouble if she didn't find the horse. Despite her panic, she had the presence of mind to kneel down and pray. She asked our Heavenly Father if He'd help her find the horse and allow her to find her way back to the cabin. Soon thereafter, a rider came up the path and gave her a ride back. Her horse had returned safe and sound and was eating grass in the pasture. That is typical of Elizabeth's faith and prayerful way. It is also indicative of her survival instincts.

I am honored and proud to be Elizabeth's mother. She's a wonderful girl who has been able to set an example that tells so many people to never give up hope. She has lived her entire life as a truly fine daughter of our Heavenly Father. She is exactly how we believe a daughter should be and act. She's considerate, strong-willed, a good student, an accomplished musician, and has a mind of her own. There is a real bond between us—and it's not always the case that a teenager wants to hang out with Mom. We genuinely like spending time together. She tells me she wants to be just like me when she grows up, and I truly appreciate hearing that—I'm not sure it'll always be that way, but for now I'll take what I can get!

Elizabeth enjoys going horseback riding, playing her harp, running, skiing, and watching movies. She loves hanging out with her brothers and sister, but she's a teenager and really *loves* being with her friends. She has an especially close bond with Mary Katherine. Despite their age difference, Elizabeth seems to enjoy being with her. Before the kidnapping, the girls shared a bedroom, arguing only when Mary Katherine's things spilled over onto Elizabeth's side of the room. That problem has since been taken care of now that they have their own rooms. Likewise, Mary Katherine looks up to her big sister and wants to be like her in every way. She learned to play the harp to follow in Elizabeth's footsteps, starting right around the same time Elizabeth learned to play—five years of age. By the time Elizabeth reached middle school, she had become a talented musician and performer. She worked very hard to master her skill, and she hopes to someday attend the Juilliard School in New York City. Anyone who really knows Elizabeth recognizes her playful, mischievous side. She has a quick wit and a great sense of humor, and if she is inspired, she can quote long passages from her favorite Sandra Bullock movie, *Miss Congeniality.*

Elizabeth has a very determined mind. If she sets her sights on something, she will get it. She has those certain qualities that separate enduring from merely getting through adversity. For us these qualities are spiritual in nature, and come from fully trusting in God. We found comfort in our prayers, certain that God would give us the strength to survive, if not triumph over, our tribulation.

Chapter 5

Ed

Have I done any good in the world today? Have I helped anyone in need? Have I cheered up the sad and made someone feel glad? If not, I have failed indeed. Has anyone's burden been lighter today, because I was willing to share? Have the sick and weary been helped on their way? When they needed my help was I there? Then wake up and do something more than dream of your mansions above. Doing good is a pleasure, a joy beyond measure, a blessing of duty and love.

—WILL L. THOMPSON

I WAS BORN OF wonderful parents. Through good and bad, they have always been there for me. My parents, Dorotha and Charles, had six children, including me. Though I was born in Utah, we moved coast to coast a few times while I was growing up. My father is a physician and completed his internship on the west coast and his residency on the east coast. This moving and the usual demands of a physician left a lot of responsibility on the shoulders of my mother. She is strong willed and has a strong faith. That faith has always been followed by action. As in James 2:20, "Faith without works is dead." She leads by an example of action.

I have felt the Lord's hand in my life many times. When my mother was pregnant with my sister Angela, I and my brothers came down with a case of the measles, which my mother then also contracted. This was of great concern to my parents. They were encouraged by other physicians to abort the pregnancy, as it was most probable that the baby would be born abnormal. Through prayer, faith, and a blessing, my mother carried that pregnancy to term. Angela was born with no complications. She is a blessing to us all.

While we were living in Washington, D.C., my father decided to take all of us on a boat trip to Tangier Island. He loved to go boating. We put into the water where the Potomac River reaches the Chesapeake. This time, the fog was so thick you could hardly see your hand in front of your face, but it was expected to burn off, so we went on our way, using a compass and nautical maps and sound buoys to plot our course. The buoys in the water helped to keep us on track. As we went farther into the channel, the air remained as thick as it was when we left, making all of us very nervous as we tried to make our way to the island. We detoured to a larger island first. We arrived safely, but realized that we would have to find another way back to avoid the fog, so we chose another route. We soon found ourselves in even more hazardous conditions, approaching a shoal where the water was especially shallow. We could have easily ripped the bottom of the boat out if my dad had made one wrong turn before reaching the outlet. After unsuccessfully trying to navigate our way out, my father suggested that we turn to prayer. We had been lost for more than an hour, wandering and fearful that we would be stranded. We took Dad's advice and prayed. Soon thereafter, we heard a bell in the distance that guided us back toward Tangier Island and home.

My father is the kind of man who never gives up on anything. He leads his family by example. Two of his favorite hymns that I remember are "Lead Kindly Light" and "Have I Done Any Good in the World Today." They epitomize his life. I'd like to believe my children feel the same way about me. My grandfather, Junius Smart, taught me to never do a job halfway. He owned a number of apartment buildings in Los Angeles. I used to help him clean the buildings and do handiwork and maintenance. A good work ethic was impressed on me from a very early age. Church was always an important factor in our lives. We rarely missed going. My grandfather taught us the importance of scripture and the role it plays in life. When I was twelve, he gave me ten dollars to memorize the following passage from the Book of Mormon:

> O, remember my son, and learn wisdom in thy youth, yea, learn in thy youth to keep the commandments of God. Yea, and cry unto God for all thy support; yea let all thy doings be unto the Lord, and whithersoever thou goest let it be in the Lord; yea let all thy thoughts be directed unto the Lord; yea let the affections for thy heart be placed upon the Lord forever. Counsel with the Lord in all thy doings, and he will direct thee for good; yea when thy liest down at night lie down unto the Lord, that he may watch over you in your sleep; and when thou risest in the morning let thy heart be full of thanks unto God; and ye do these things, ye shall be lifted up at the last day.
>
> —ALMA 37:35–37

That passage left an indelible mark on me. It speaks to how important prayer is and to being thankful for what you have. When

Elizabeth was taken, it was one of the passages that offered Lois and me much comfort. How could I have ever known at age twelve that my grandpa was passing on scripture that would impact me deeply in my time of need?

Like most young men of our faith, I went on a mission when I was nineteen years old to serve the Lord by sharing the gospel of the Church of Jesus Christ of Latter-Day Saints. I spent two years in Arizona spreading the word of God. While on my mission, I shared the principles of the gospel as we understand it, and what it meant to me in my life. It was important for me to show people that they had to have their own personal relationship with God. Prayer is a large part of those teachings. People have to find out on their own what that means for them. For us, prayer needs to be personalized. We pray as if we are actually speaking to the deity—with reverence. It's something from your heart.

I, like everyone, make choices in life, both good and bad. The faith I've developed over the years has been a result of the example set before me and my personal experience. Life, for the most part, has truly been sweet to me. I have been tremendously blessed with a wonderful family, an extraordinary life and wife, and wonderful parents and parents-in-law. My family means everything to me. It always has and always will.

Chapter 6

When ye are in the service of your fellow beings,
you are only in the service of your God.

—MOSIAH 2:17

I<small>N THE DAYS</small> before the kidnapping, we were driving in the car together and saw people on the street who seemed down on their luck. They looked homeless. We talked about who these people were and where they had come from. What had happened in their lives that they had come to this point? Wasn't there anyone in this world who loved and cared for these people? We talked about how we could make this a better world for them and what we could do to help lighten their load. We talked about what a harsh world it can be and just how easy it is to lose everything. In a minute, life can change.

In our effort to reach out to these people, it was not unusual for us to hire a local homeless person to do a little yard work around our home. We have done that for years. That is how we met Brian David Mitchell. Lois, Charles, Elizabeth, Andrew, Edward, Mary Katherine, and William first came upon him as he was panhandling in front of a local mall. Lois handed him five dollars and asked him if he was looking for work. He was very clean-cut and dressed in clean clothes. He did not appear to be homeless. Lois gave him our telephone number and told him to speak to Ed. We had Mitchell to the house only that one time. He came for four or five hours. He mostly worked on the roof with Ed, who struck up limited conversation. He said his name was "Immanuel," though Ed was certain that was not his given name. He saw the children for only a few minutes that day—and as far as we know, until the morning of June 5, 2002, that was the only time he had ever been to our home.

Who are we to judge anyone? We all make mistakes. Sometimes people just need a fresh start to get things moving in a positive direction again. That's why we have hired the homeless over the years. We believe that there are far more good than evil people out there. Those who are having a hard time still find the will to carry on and persevere. They want to do something good. We never questioned where anyone came from or if they had a checkered past. Maybe we should have, but we didn't. We brought these day workers home but never let them inside the house. Our children had very little, if any, contact with them. They usually helped for a few hours doing yard work and landscaping.

We hired Richard Ricci, who was not homeless, in March 2001 for some long-term projects at the suggestion of a contractor friend who had picked up his name from a job referral service. The contractor wasn't able to use him because his staff was primarily Spanish-speaking and Ricci spoke only English. The contractor said Ricci seemed to be a capable worker, so we thought we'd give him a try.

At our suggestion, Ricci initially went to our neighbor's home, since they also needed work done around their house. During the time of his employment there, someone (we later learned it was Ricci) broke into their home late at night. No one realized they'd been robbed until the next morning. Money and jewelry were missing, but the police couldn't find a connection to anyone who'd recently been in the house. After finishing his work with our neighbors, Richard started working for us on a day-by-day basis. He was always likable, always asking how we were, how our weekend was. Small talk. He really couldn't do the kind of finish work we needed around the house, but he was always a willing candidate. We decided to start him out on yard work.

After his first week on the job, Ricci started talking about buying a car. He had been getting a ride to work every day from his girlfriend. We had a 1990 Jeep Cherokee we were trying to sell, and after talking it over, we decided to give Ricci the car in exchange for his work. We wrote up a contract that specified he was to work forty hours a week, a certain portion of which would go toward the purchase of the Jeep. He agreed to work five days a week. Ed helped take care of the registration and insurance and then gave him the Jeep. When Richard didn't show up to work for several days, we both had a bad feeling, so we decided to find Ricci and get the Jeep back. We want to trust that people are basically good, but it seemed that the faith and trust we had put in him had been misplaced.

Ed found Ricci and took the car back home. A few days later, Ricci showed up for work and it appeared as if everything was back on track. We gave him back the Jeep, hopeful that he was not taking advantage of our kindness. But this time we put our name down on the title as lienholders. Although he could have not shown up again, Ricci reached out to us and came back, worked, and finished paying off the car. We were relieved that this time he had kept his word. One of his jobs was painting the hallway in the entry of our home, so there was no way we could fail to interact with him. He was always talking about his girlfriend, Angela, and how they wanted to get married. Lois felt somewhat uncomfortable having him or any virtual stranger in our home, especially around the children. Ricci was an especially friendly guy who talked to our sons about motorcycles and snowmobiles—but still, something seemed out of place.

Three months after we hired Ricci, Lois noticed that she was missing a bracelet. It was a very beautiful and expensive bracelet, but it was particularly valuable to Lois for sentimental reasons. When it was discovered to be missing, it didn't matter who was working in the home. Everyone was excused from their jobs, including Richard Ricci. We called the police and gave a detailed report, including the names of all workers who had been at our home in recent weeks. The police assured us they would check out people who had been working for us at the time—but later they reported that they had found nothing. Then we discovered that there were many other items missing.

Ed did a little investigative work on his own to see if he could turn up anything in Ricci's background. It wasn't until after Elizabeth was kidnapped that we discovered he was a convicted felon. How could this not have surfaced in the police investigations? We later learned that Ricci had been released from jail less than a year before he came to work for us. He had been sentenced to twenty-eight years in prison for shooting a police officer following a robbery. We didn't know any of this when we hired him. The police had checked out Ricci, but for a second time (the first was when our neighbors were robbed) they came up with none of this, which in hindsight was an ironic precursor of the investigation into Elizabeth's kidnapping.

Ricci worked for us for approximately three months. He was in and out of the house all the time. The children knew him, and he knew our home. He knew where spare keys were hanging, he had access to the house, and he knew that we had an alarm system we never used. He called us in September 2001 to ask whether the title for the Jeep had been sent to us. It had come in mid-July, but at the time we didn't know where to find him or how to forward it. Ed suggested he come by the house to pick it up. When Ricci arrived, he made a point of adamantly denying stealing Lois's bracelet, even going so far as to tell us that he went to the police station to take a polygraph test to prove his innocence. We appreciated this attempt to ease our minds, but something inside told us he wasn't completely innocent.

That was the last time we saw Richard Ricci. His name was never uttered in our home again until after Elizabeth was kidnapped.

Chapter 7

Lois

*Wherefore, be of good cheer, and do not fear, for I the Lord
am with you and will stand by you . . .*

—D&C 68:6

Our family was exhausted on the night Elizabeth was taken. Sadly, my father had passed away a few days before. He had never been sick a day in his life, but at the end of February 2002 he was diagnosed with a brain tumor. The doctors hadn't given him a good prognosis, but they believed he had longer than the three months he actually had left to live. I spent every day of those three months at his side, doing whatever I could to offer my mother and him help, peace, and comfort. He had always been strong and hardworking. He was the picture of health and very active until those last months.

Dad was a devoted spiritual leader and was called to be a Temple president in the Philippines when he was in his seventies. Dad loved doing church work, just as he loved to get out on his property and shovel, plant trees, and tend to his flowers to keep himself busy. My parents' home was an oasis for their entire family (especially for their fifty-one grandchildren), and we often gathered to have parties there. All of our children loved my father, but Elizabeth and Mary Katherine had very special connections with him. My father always enjoyed planting his garden in the spring, but when he became too ill to plant, the girls offered to do it for him. They planted corn and peas just a few weeks before he died. I know it meant so much to him that they were able to do that.

It was during the 2002 Winter Olympics in Salt Lake City that we first noticed my father was sleeping a lot more than usual, and that he had started walking with a bit of a shuffle and would occasionally stumble. The family kept thinking it was just old age setting in and surely nothing to be too worried about. But when his difficulties continued, we decided it was time to take him to the doctor, thinking that maybe he had developed diabetes or something else treatable. It never occurred to us that our patriarch was seriously ill. It took several weeks before the doctors diagnosed the brain tumor. They felt the situation was severe enough to operate on him as soon as possible. Before they did so, my sister was able to fly in from her home in Virginia, and we spent the weekend together as a family, fasting and praying in a conference room in the hospital. There were seventy people altogether, praying for my father.

Dad had an incredible memory. He never forgot a thing. Just before he went for his surgery a few days later, he was beautifully reciting passages of poetry from "Little Boy Blue," "The Highwayman," and "Gunga Din." Afterward, he was remarkably coherent and could communicate easily. We felt confident that he was going to make it. Though still in the intensive-care unit, he seemed to be doing great. We all thought that he was going to recover and live another twenty years.

That optimism faded a bit a few hours later when Dad slipped into a comalike state. Unless he started to show improvement, the hospital had to release him. We agreed it was better for him to go home. We were uncertain as to the best way to take care of him there, but that is where we knew he would want to be. Ed's father, a cancer specialist, helped us with the arrangements for taking care of him at home. Despite our concerns, Dad improved with every passing day. He could sit up and feed himself, and all indications were that he was on the road to recovery. By the end of May, however, Dad took an unexpected turn for the worse. Something changed. We had a sense that his time had come. For some inexplicable reason, my father needed to pass on.

My father was a protector in every sense of the word. When I was in my twenties and working as a first-grade teacher, I would sometimes have to work late, and my father would meet me in the parking lot of the school and follow me in his car just to make sure I made it home safely. That's the kind of dad he was. Though we had no way of knowing it at the time, my father had to pass on when he did so that he could protect Elizabeth. He died on May 28. His funeral was June 3. At his service, Elizabeth and Mary Katherine played a duet on their harps of one of Dad's favorite songs, "Silent Night." My father's death had a profound impact on me—though I would barely have time to recognize just how important an event it would be after Elizabeth was abducted. Two days after we buried Dad, on the morning of June 5, Elizabeth too was gone.

The evening of June 4, 2002, Elizabeth was scheduled to play her harp at an awards ceremony for Bryant Intermediate School, her junior high. It was the year-end awards program, where Elizabeth accepted several awards for her outstanding work.

Around five o'clock that afternoon, Ed was driving home from work and pulled onto our street, where he saw Elizabeth and Mary Katherine jogging. Elizabeth was training for the high school cross-country track team, which she planned to join in the fall. He stopped to say hello and ask where they were going. They were on their way to run around the reservoir near our home. They asked for a ride over, and he jokingly told them that if they were going for a jog, they were actually supposed to do it! "If you want to be a track star, Elizabeth, you'd better get going," he said, and sent them on their way.

Everything seemed so rushed that night. We always ate at six o'clock. By six-fifteen, Elizabeth still was not home and we were eating dinner. We were supposed to be at her school by quarter to seven. I became concerned that if we were late to the ceremony, Elizabeth would be unable to play her harp as scheduled—and I was right. Elizabeth missed her performance. However, we managed to make it to school in time for Elizabeth to receive her awards that night, and we all beamed with pride each time she came off the stage.

Since I had frequently been away from home spending time with my father, I was looking forward to spending lots of quality time with my family that summer. Elizabeth had been asking if she could go for three or four days with her friend's family on vacation the day after school let out. I was reluctant to say yes. I had missed being with my children while my father was ill, and I didn't feel it was necessary to allow Elizabeth to go away. I wanted her home, and besides, we were planning to go on our own family vacation later that month. But she wanted to go so badly that Ed and I agreed to talk it over, and just before bed we told Elizabeth she could plan to go with her friend. We said good night. That was the last conversation we had before she was kidnapped.

Chapter 8

ED

Trust in the Lord with all thine heart; and lean not unto thine own understanding. In all ways acknowledge Him and He shall direct thy paths.

—PROVERBS 3:5–6

EARLIER THAT NIGHT Lois had prepared a special dinner for everyone as a way to get back to our family unity. There had been so much going on with her father's illness that we just wanted to regroup. Sit-down dinners are important to us, because that is the only real daily family time we have together. It is the time when we can gauge how the family is doing and hear about one another's day. Lois opened the tall kitchen window over the sink to get some air flowing because she had accidentally burned the potatoes. It is a fairly narrow window, about sixteen and a half inches wide. It cranks open, and it has a screen. I am certain the window was still cranked open when we went to bed, since we used to leave windows open all the time. We live at the end of a cul-de-sac, and we never felt it was unsafe to leave a window open.

When we returned home from the awards ceremony, Lois asked me to check the doors and make certain they were all locked. I hadn't yet taken the harp out of the car, so I knew I had to go out to the garage anyway to carry it into the house. Before I closed things up, we gathered to have our nightly family prayers. I said good night to the children and went off to secure the house. I checked the front double doors, the sliding doors off the kitchen, and the back door, then I headed into the garage to make sure that the door was secure. It had been open most of the day with a piece of cardboard obstructing the laser, keeping the door from closing. I went back to check the doors on the mezzanine, which were hardly ever used. This might sound like a lot of checking, but the nightly routine took only a few minutes. We thought all of our doors had chimes as part of the security system. Unbeknownst to us, they did not—two doors and the back kitchen door were not functioning properly. These doors were missing the magnets that made contact to make the doors chime.

At the time, we were thinking of moving permanently to our cabin, so our house was up for sale. The children really love being up there, where they can go outdoors and do the activities that they love—like skiing, snowboarding, mountain biking, and hiking. We liked the idea because we wanted to keep our family tight and together. I was working nonstop and felt it was time to reevaluate our priorities. It felt as if we were all moving so fast through life, and we wanted to slow down a little and enjoy the time we had together while the children were still home. It wasn't so much the cabin that was the pull; it was the idea of being in a place that had a slower pace.

At about ten-thirty Lois and I finished talking with Elizabeth about her trip. We kissed her good night, and she went off to bed wearing her favorite red silk pajamas. Charles had been up working on a paper for school and went to sleep around midnight. We were all exhausted from the funeral and from the awards ceremony. Our children were especially worn out from all the running around we'd been doing and from staying up later than usual several nights in a row. William, our baby, wound up sleeping with us in our room.

When Mary Katherine came into our room and told us that Elizabeth was gone, I thought she had just had a bad dream—until she told us Elizabeth had been taken at gunpoint. When Mary Katherine said, "You won't find her. She's gone," I could tell she was genuinely terrified. I jumped out of bed and started checking all the bedrooms, starting with hers. Elizabeth wasn't there. Elizabeth had been asking us for her own bedroom, and I thought that perhaps she was sleeping in the bed in the guest room on the main floor. Sometimes she'd even sleep in William's room, especially on the nights he slept in our room.

All I could think as I was running around the house was "Is this really happening?" Lois turned on all the lights in the kitchen. That's when I heard her scream for me to call the police. Lois and I were standing in the kitchen, Mary Katherine trailing us, still wrapped in her blanket. She whispered, "You're not going to find her. She's not here." The horror of what was happening was incomprehensible, yet it was quickly seeping in that our daughter had been taken from us. I was consumed with thoughts of how someone got in and out of the house without us hearing any sign of him, no creaking step, no door chime.

I called 911 at 4:01 A.M. and explained that someone had broken into our home and had taken our daughter. (Some reports in the media have said that I called 911 after I called several friends, but phone records show that my 911 call was placed first.) My parents were out of town, so the first phone call I made after that was to our home teacher, a very close friend who lives nearby. A home teacher is a member of a ward who is assigned to check on a family and is there to be a source of support and help in any way a family might need. This man is someone our whole family is very close with. We were definitely in need of his help. Lois called her mother, then we placed calls to some of our close friends, neighbors, and other members of our ward. Twelve minutes after my call to 911, the police arrived. Our first friends arrived around 4:15.

One of our neighbors had been the victim of an attempted abduction in 1992. I am not sure why this went through my mind, but I instinctively ran to their house and pounded on the front door. I wanted to be certain that none of their girls had been taken with Elizabeth. It took what seemed like forever for them to answer. When they did, I explained that Elizabeth had been kidnapped and I wanted to be certain that they checked on their children. I ran back to our house, got on the phone, and called more family members and friends, ward members—and anyone else I could think of—to start to pull together several search teams.

My brother Tom had been in a deep sleep induced by a sleeping pill when he received my first phone call. He was groggy, didn't register what I was telling him, and didn't even realize what time it was (afterward, he mistakenly thought that I had phoned him at 3:30). Later, when Tom still hadn't arrived at our home, I phoned again and got his wife and explained the situation. She roused Tom from his sleep. Tom is a photographer for *The Deseret News* in Salt Lake. I really wanted him to be there to help, especially since he had excellent connections with the media and I knew he could get Elizabeth's photo circulated within minutes. Tom arrived around thirty or forty minutes later and collected several family pictures we had of Elizabeth. Joy Gough, a local photographer, had taken several photos of Elizabeth playing the harp the summer before. These photographs were included in the photos Tom got to the news wire services and posted on the Internet. By early morning, Elizabeth's photos had been placed in every medium imaginable.

By then our neighborhood had been alerted that an intruder had broken into our home and Elizabeth was missing. The news of her disappearance had quickly traveled through the streets of Federal Heights and beyond. The police separated Lois from me and took Mary Katherine to another floor so that her recollection of what had happened would not be tainted in any way. I stood in the kitchen with our home teacher and some other friends from the ward, and together we placed calls to our entire ward directory to enlist help. Mary Katherine was alone with the police. Lois was concerned for her, since she was clearly traumatized, and asked her mother and sister, who were now at our home, to sit with Mary Katherine to comfort her.

I remember feeling as if the police didn't have control over the situation. It was as if they were waiting for something to happen or someone to come and tell them what to do. I was bothered that they weren't out there looking for my daughter. By the time my brother David tried to get into our home, less than an hour after I called 911, the police wouldn't let him up because there were too many people in the house. The house had not yet been sealed as a crime scene, which was confusing and troubling to us. Looking back, this turned out to be a huge oversight on the part of the police. It wasn't until Sergeant Don Bell showed up that the house was finally secured.

By six o'clock that morning, friends were canvassing the neighborhood, knocking on every door and asking if anyone had seen or heard anything that might lend a clue in helping to find Elizabeth. One neighbor said he thought he had heard a female voice crying out around two in the morning. At the time, we didn't know if the voice was Elizabeth's. It turned out to be the voice of a girl traveling with a group of young motorcyclists. The neighbor had heard dogs barking and checked on his dog to make sure everything was okay. When nothing suspicious turned up, he went back to bed.

Around 6:30 in the morning, Lois, Charles, Andrew, and I got dressed and were taken to the police station. The police had informed me that we would have to go in for questioning. As the police chief would later say, "Everyone is a suspect." Lois and I were taken in one police car, and Charles and Andrew in another. Lois and I were told not to speak to each other. Mary Katherine would later be taken to the Children's Justice Center, escorted by Lois's mother and sister. William and Edward went to a neighbor's home. When we arrived at the station, Lois and I were separated for questioning. Charles and Andrew were being questioned in another room. We were being monitored by video cameras. Lois wanted to get through whatever we needed to do and go home to be there for Elizabeth. We had nothing to hide. I was anxious because I felt time was slipping away and I simply wanted to get out of the station and look for Elizabeth.

When the police started questioning us, their first goal was to try and get a handle on who Elizabeth Smart was. What kind of girl was she? Did she have a boyfriend? Was she promiscuous? Did she experiment with drugs? Was she into the occult? Could she have run away? How was her relationship with her mom and me? How did she get along with her brothers? Did she spend a lot of time on the Internet? Fingers were quickly pointed in the direction of the victim. As frustrating as those questions were, they were a necessary part of the investigation, because the truth is, often those questions are relevant to the case. Every year, 203,900 children are abducted by family members and more than 200,000 missing kids are runaways.

When it came to Elizabeth, none of those possibilities was at all true. She was a very young fourteen-year-old. To make matters worse, our other children were also closely scrutinized. Charles was brought in for questioning, and he too was barraged by insulting personal attacks. "Did you kill your sister?" "Did a friend of yours kill your sister?" The disappearance was hard enough, but this questioning made it worse. We were in complete shock. We were grieving and feeling a kind of pain that is indescribable, and the allegations made during questioning were insufferable. As if our world hadn't been rocked already by Elizabeth's disappearance, they tried to rip apart everything we held near and dear. Our marriage, our children, our integrity, our faith—all of it was put to question after Elizabeth's kidnapping.

Several hours had passed from the time Mary Katherine awoke Lois and me to when Don Bell officially turned our home into a crime scene—at 6:54 that morning, nearly six hours after Elizabeth went to bed and nearly three hours after my call to 911. People were buzzing all over our home, street, and neighborhood. Police would later describe allowing all of those people into the home as a giant mistake on their part. Unfortunately, so many people had been through the house by the time they sealed the scene that any clues or evidence that may have been left behind were thought to be tainted.

Until that morning, I had no awareness of the Rachael Alert, which is essentially what has come to be called the Amber Alert. Created in 1996, the Amber Alert stands as a legacy to nine-year-old Amber Hagerman, who was kidnapped while riding her bicycle in broad daylight and was later found brutally murdered. This innovative early warning system utilizes the Emergency Alert System (EAS), formerly known as the Emergency Broadcast System, which allows broadcasters and law-enforcement agencies to distribute urgent information once it is confirmed that a child has been abducted. These bulletins can contain descriptions of the abducted child, the suspected abductor, and the suspect's vehicle. Within hours, television stations and various cable networks begin running "crawls" on their transmissions containing information about the crime, and since then, some states employ traffic billboards to disseminate information to drivers. Radio stations play an important part as well, interrupting local programming to announce alerts. By eight o'clock in the morning, the Rachael Alert on Elizabeth had gone out.

The media converged on our front yard early that morning. My sister Angela called two close friends, Ruth Todd and Kim Johnson, local Salt Lake City news anchors whose interest in finding Elizabeth went beyond simply "getting the story." They were definitely part of the original thrust that quickly pushed this local kidnapping into national news. We are so grateful for the kind consideration those women gave to our family that morning and all during Elizabeth's disappearance. When the morning news came on, Elizabeth was the lead story on every station. Morning commuters heard the news that Salt Lake was missing one of its children.

The police brought us to my parents' home by about nine o'clock that morning. My parents had arrived home from Lake Powell by this time. We weren't able to go to our house, because it had been sealed as a crime scene. We decided to assemble our own search team. Our oldest son Charles went on a search with our home teacher, driving around our neighborhood and through the hillsides and foothills of the area.

Everything felt surreal. I was in a total state of disbelief. Lois was shaking uncontrollably—it was painful for me to see my wife like that, because she is the strongest woman I know. It might have appeared that I was the strong, fearless patriarch of our family, but we both had to be strong and rely on each other in our ups and downs. We were in a situation that we had never anticipated. We could never have gotten through this nightmare without each other.

These are the types of situations that destroy marriages and families. But our marriage became stronger, our relationship grew stronger, and our family became closer. We both realized that we wouldn't have been able to survive had it not been for the strength we brought to each other. There were plenty of days when if one of us felt blue, the other would buoy up. We got through this by being best friends. There is nothing—absolutely nothing—that helped us more than relying on each other and believing that we had the necessary faith and trust in God. If we hadn't stayed positive about the outcome or outlook of the situation, that would have directly impacted and affected our other children. Even though Elizabeth was missing, we had a family to look after and be there for. Lois realized that necessity long before I did.

The statistics are staggering when it comes to a crime such as Elizabeth's abduction. There are 800,000 missing-children cases a year in this country, or about two thousand children a day. Forty-eight percent of the time a child goes missing, particularly a white girl from an upper-middle-class family, the culprit is a close family member or friend. Lois and I couldn't imagine who would do something like this—certainly not anyone in our immediate family. No one came to mind.

It was reported that this was considered to be the most publicized kidnapping since the Lindbergh case. The summer of 2002 became the summer of missing children, with Elizabeth just one of many. Statistically there were no more kidnappings than usual that summer, just a heightened awareness because of the massive media coverage. That new awareness brought to light the need to have a unified nationwide alert system to aid families of missing children in their search—something both Lois and I became extremely passionate about while Elizabeth was gone, and are even more so now that she is home.

It is important to note that as we write this book, one year after Elizabeth was kidnapped, we have heard very little about missing children, even though we know there are just as many families as ever out there who are in the same painful situation we were in.

The hours were passing, and still no sign of Elizabeth. Later that afternoon, a member of our ward phoned to tell me about a wonderful organization, the Laura Recovery Center Foundation. Based in Friendswood, Texas, the Laura Foundation was established by members of the Friendswood community after twelve-year-old Laura Kate Smither was abducted near her home on April 3, 1997. A nationwide search was immediately launched, and more than six thousand volunteers searched round-the-clock until her body was recovered some seventeen days later. Today, the Foundation functions as a volunteer response team, conducting ground searches and distributing educational materials such as the *Laura Recovery Center Manual.* The manual serves as a comprehensive text containing everything people need to know in dealing with abductions, from organizing search patterns to effective phone bank operations. In 2002 alone, the Laura Recovery Center helped 160 families search for a missing child. The sister of one of the Foundation's volunteers lived near us. She was at our service almost immediately upon hearing the news about Elizabeth. The same day, other volunteers flew to Salt Lake to help set up the Elizabeth Smart Search Center. The Abby and Jennifer Recovery Foundation, Inc. also came from Grand Junction, Colorado, to offer its assistance and was just as helpful as the Laura Foundation. The Abby and Jennifer Recovery Foundation handled most of the out-of-city searches, which meant coordinating airplanes and helicopters for aerial searches, as well as organizing the forest teams and the mountain searches. They did an excellent job managing information coming in and going out as a result of their search efforts.

Initiating the search teams became very important. Volunteers and offers to help were pouring in. We knew every passing hour meant that Elizabeth was getting farther and farther from our reach. A neighbor's son-in-law helped to quickly get the Elizabeth Smart Web page up and running, and my brother David took over the day-to-day operation. David then spent many hours developing it into an interactive site that allowed searchers to log their progress and make note of any significant developments. It allowed people to get instant updates on the case and to send in any information about Elizabeth's disappearance. Considered to be very progressive, it will be used as a prototype for future kidnapping and missing-children situations, and today the National Center for Missing and Exploited Children is considering using it with other cases. The site at one point was receiving more than one million hits a day. Unable to handle the load, Intel later donated a host site to us. People wrote to the site asking for more frequent updates. They wanted up-to-the-minute information. Search information that offered instructions on how to search and what to do with the information was posted on the Web site. The site organized people from all over to help in our efforts to look for Elizabeth.

Chapter 9

He is always near me, though I do not see Him there.
And because He loves me dearly, I am in His watchful care.

—"If the Savior Stood Beside Me,"
words and music by Sally DeFord

THE NIGHT ELIZABETH was kidnapped, we later learned, she had
been forced to march up Lime Kiln Gulch to Dry Creek Canyon, a
three-mile hike from our home. Brian David Mitchell told her that
he would kill her family if she didn't do what he said. All the way up
the canyon, he told her that God had commanded him to take her.
Elizabeth hadn't yet registered who this man was. She had seen him
for only a few minutes when she first met him at the crosswalk

outside the mall, and then briefly at our home. Brian looked totally different; he now had a long beard and long hair, but Elizabeth somehow gradually was able to make the connection. "Didn't you help my dad do some work on the roof? Why are you doing this to me?" Elizabeth asked. Brian repeated, "God has commanded me to do this." That's all he would say. The hike took many hours, with a difficult steep incline before they reached the top of the canyon. It was dark, and the night air was chilly. Elizabeth was still wearing her red silk pajamas and the pair of running shoes she had been allowed to take.

It appeared that Brian had spent months preparing for the kidnapping. He was carefully building a campsite that was mostly hidden by the trees and the thick brush of the mountains behind our home. He was still working on the site after he kidnapped Elizabeth. The shelter was a trench about twenty feet long, with logs for a roof, laid over with thick plastic garbage bags and a tarp and camouflaged with dirt, leaves, and sticks on top. This structure was not where Elizabeth was held captive for two months; rather, it was in a tent next to it, tethered between two trees on a cable that ran along a line, allowing her some movement, but only as far as the cable reached. Needless to say, she had no privacy.

She was treated like a slave, forced to wait on Brian and Wanda like a servant. They had given Elizabeth a paring knife to use when she cut vegetables. On many occasions when she was able, she tried to use the small knife to cut through the metal cable, but she was able to shred only the plastic covering and not the cable itself. Wanda and Brian argued all the time, and were constantly ranting and raving. During one argument, Elizabeth realized that Brian had forgotten to connect her to her cable. Seizing the opportunity, she tried to escape, but Brian immediately saw her trying to run. "Where do you think you're going?" he said, catching her. Elizabeth, who had been a very good runner before she was taken, simply didn't have the strength to outrun Brian; whereas Brian was somewhat of a health fanatic and exercised constantly to keep fit.

As search teams combed the area, Elizabeth later said, she could hear the sound of people calling her name, especially one of her uncles, whose voice was familiar and seemed very close. Hundreds of people were within hailing distance, but she was unable to cry out for help, unable to escape. Brian brandished his knife to remind Elizabeth what he was capable of doing. She was profoundly frightened, convinced that Brian would hurt her or her family if she disobeyed his orders to keep quiet. She was right there—but no one knew just how close. She may as well have been invisible.

Helicopters scanned the terrain behind our house, and volunteers arrived from Montana with bloodhound teams that would sniff the entire area. We had given searchers clothes, pillowcases, and other items with Elizabeth's scent. None of the search dog teams were able to pick up a scent that led very far. One dog caught a scent just outside our home and followed it up a trail behind our house until it stopped at the upper road. We now realize that this trail was correct, but why the dogs never picked up a scent that continued up the hill behind our home is still baffling to us—Elizabeth and Brian walked the entire way up the canyon. One theory had been that Elizabeth may have been put into a car that had been waiting to take her away. For days, search groups headed up every trailhead near our home, searching the hills for a clue.

Posters with Elizabeth's image and the words "Pray For Me" and "Missing" across the top started going up all over Salt Lake City. Ed's sister Angela went to a nearby Kinko's and quickly printed up thousands of posters. A $10,000 reward was already being offered by the Salt Lake police for anyone with information leading to Elizabeth's return.

We wanted the police to expand the search beyond Salt Lake, beyond Utah, and into neighboring states, such as Wyoming, Idaho, and even Oregon, where two teenage girls had been abducted and killed earlier in the year. The Utah Missing Persons Clearinghouse was a big help, distributing several hundred fliers to law-enforcement and schools in neighboring states. The word was spreading, and our local story was quickly turning into national news. We are particularly indebted to a local printer who donated hundreds of thousands of copies of the flier that was seen around the country.

On the afternoon of June 5, Ed decided to face the media for the first time after Elizabeth was reported missing to give the first of what would become twice-daily press conferences. Unable to hold his head up, begging and pleading with whoever had taken Elizabeth to bring her home.

"Elizabeth, if you're out there, we're doing everything we possibly can to help you. We love you. We want you to come home safely to us.

"To the person who has our daughter, I can't imagine why you took her to begin with. There is no reason that you should have taken her. Please let her go. Please! Elizabeth! Elizabeth!"

He tried to choke back his tears, but his grief was obvious and painful for everyone who watched Ed that afternoon.

We were all traumatized. The police had informed us that the first twenty-four hours are the most crucial in searching for a missing child. Most children abducted by strangers are victims of pedophiles, and most often if the abductor intends to murder their victim, they will do so in the first three hours. If a kidnapper is seeking ransom, there is usually some contact from the kidnapper within the first twenty-four hours. We had heard nothing, but we were certain Elizabeth was out there somewhere. Unable to sleep, we fasted, prayed, and kept searching for Elizabeth.

Our other daughter, Mary Katherine, the other victim and the only witness to this crime, was being questioned about what she saw. Police and investigators spent much of the early-morning hours trying to glean as much information as they could from our traumatized daughter. By nine o'clock, more than one hundred people were searching for Elizabeth, including family, friends, ward members, law-enforcement officials, and other Salt Lake Good Samaritans. The only information they had was the description Mary Katherine offered of a white man about five feet eight. He was wearing a light-colored jacket and a white golf-style hat pulled over his eyes. He was armed with what Mary Katherine believed to be a gun. Mary Katherine loved her sister dearly. She would have done anything to help bring her home, speaking openly to the police and trying to give as many details as she could remember. It was difficult for her to talk about the experience, but she spoke to whoever needed to garner information from her.

There are so many things that come up after a child is abducted that are not part of parents' initial comprehension. The National Center for Missing and Exploited Children instituted the Team Adam Project (named for John Walsh's son, who was kidnapped and killed) as a team specializing in abductions. When a child goes missing, his or her information goes to a national information bank that services law-enforcement agencies and the FBI. Team Adam and Project Alert have teams of specialists to help assess the situation. They can play a key role in helping families get through the experience. The organization has incredible teams of experts trained with amazing resources, available for anyone who goes through a missing-child crisis. However, many law-enforcement agencies are unaware of how to handle missing-children cases. Organizing a search, dealing with the media, handling the investigation—how in the world does a family know where to begin when they aren't thinking clearly from the very beginning?

Our family and some of our close friends became extremely involved in the Elizabeth Smart Search Center, organizing many of the local donations we needed to keep the center running and the volunteers working. If it was too hot to stand in the sun, they made sure canopies were brought in. Numerous stories were relayed to us about the many times the phone would ring at the center and it would be someone offering whatever we needed at that moment free of charge: food, water, thousands of posters, flashlights, batteries, communication devices, and so on. There were so many acts of such kindness. People were hand-making buttons with Elizabeth's image and a caption that said, "Pray for me." People started to wear light blue ribbons on their lapels. When Elizabeth missed her graduation from junior high school, her teachers and friends made a sign out of blue ribbons and tied it to the chain-link fence; it read, "We ♡ You Liz." Eventually companies offered to manufacture the buttons and ribbons for us. Charles, in a sign of solidarity and hope for his sister, wore three blue ribbons around his wrist with a heart-shaped bead on each. He wore the ribbons until Elizabeth came home, and then for a few months after, until they became so frayed and worn that he finally cut them off at the one-year anniversary of Elizabeth's kidnapping. He even wore a button on his tuxedo lapel when he attended the junior prom.

We made a point of trying to get to the search center every day to thank the volunteers, but we want to be sure that everyone who donated their time, supplies, and services knows how truly grateful we are for all you did. You will never know the depth of our appreciation. Your generosity overflowed, and our hearts were deeply touched by all of you.

Within the first week, an additional $250,000 reward was announced, raised from private donations. The reward would be given to any person with information leading to the rescue of our daughter. Their generous contributions were one of our greatest blessings. Their gift made possible what we could not do on our own. Police Chief Rick Dinse appointed Don Bell to head up the investigation, along with Salt Lake law-enforcement officials and members of the FBI.

Shriner's Hospital was the first official search center site to be set up after Elizabeth's disappearance. Shriner's Hospital has always been kind to our community, and their allowing us to set up the search center there was very generous. Located just down the road from our house, it had the available space to handle the onslaught of volunteers who came by to help. The morning of June 6, we stopped by to thank everyone who'd interrupted their lives to aid our search. It had been only twenty-four hours, but it felt as if a lifetime had passed. We knew in our hearts that this was the best way we could bring Elizabeth home. As gut-wrenching as it was, we had to keep the search parties going out and the volunteers coming in. We had to be there to support those who came out to give so generously of their time.

The first few days always began with appearances on the morning talk shows. We tried to maintain our composure morning after morning as we made a national plea for the person or persons who had our daughter to bring her home. The morning of June 6, Lois fell apart during an interview on the *Today* show. Normally a pillar of strength, the thought of Elizabeth being lost was more than she could bear, but she was willing to go through anything to bring Elizabeth home. Together we were two halves of a complete whole. The balance worked for us—it helped save our spirits.

Since we had never had a need for a publicist prior to the kidnapping, it was hard to imagine that Elizabeth's abduction warranted hiring one. Yet the media coverage became so dense, the family simply could not handle the load. People were calling for interviews, statements, exclusives, and appearances. Neither of us had the savvy to understand how to make the media work to help us in our situation, but we certainly knew we couldn't bring Elizabeth home without it. We found true friends in Chris Thomas and the Intrepid Group, a public relations firm based in Salt Lake City, which had been referred to our family through Tom. The first few months were donated free of charge, but when the workload became a full-time job, Chris was handed the account. He managed our media, sometimes eighteen hours a day, for nine months—until Elizabeth came home.

Chris played a very important role in helping direct our family, especially Ed, through the media frenzy that seemed to be feeding on our misfortune. He was with our family so often that Lois came to refer to him as her fifth son. Ed felt as if he had found another brother in Chris. He acted as a buffer between the press and our family. There were many times that Ed simply wasn't able to face the cameras. Chris was there for the family. Chris understood the importance of working the press to keep the search for Elizabeth alive. He protected all of us from the media when sleep deprivation and our emotions became burdensome and we stopped making sense. He felt as if the Lord had sent him to help us—and looking back, he was a tremendous help. Chris prepared us to go in front of the media, working with focus points we had prepared beforehand during family meetings. He helped Ed focus on the message he needed to get out in his two-minute segments on the talk shows or during the daily press conferences.

Investigators continued to interview Mary Katherine, being extremely cautious not to push too hard so that she didn't have to relive the horror of witnessing her sister being stolen. Our family was deeply concerned for her well-being. We had received helpful advice from trauma counselors about how to reduce the stress she might have been feeling in coming up with details of that fateful night. There was a chance that she would completely shut down from too much questioning, rendering her unable to recall any specific details.

Mary Katherine stood firmly by her story of what happened the night that Elizabeth was taken. At one point, a specialist tried to hypnotize her—but still she wouldn't budge from what she saw. Now, it is important to point out that what Mary Katherine recalled was not necessarily what happened. The police were careful to avoid letting all of the information about the break-in go public. Mary Katherine believed that she saw a man take Elizabeth at gunpoint. Initially, I understood that he tapped Mary Katherine on the shoulder, and when she turned over she saw Brian looking at her nightstand. Then she saw Brian pull out what she believed to be a gun and point it at Elizabeth. Elizabeth said, "Why are you doing this?" Mary Katherine thought she heard Brian say "ransom" or "hostage." Elizabeth stubbed her toe in the darkness of the bedroom and said, "Ouch." She heard Brian say to Elizabeth, "Be quiet or I am going to kill you." At this point Mary Katherine was feigning sleep. Brian told Elizabeth to get some shoes. For a moment a light went on in the closet where Elizabeth would put on her running shoes. Mary Katherine believes that Brian walked with Elizabeth down the hallway and looked into her brothers' bedrooms. They walked down the stairs and out of the house through the back door. Mary Katherine never knew which door they went out. A few seconds after that, she heard Elizabeth say "ouch" a second time; she believed Elizabeth had fallen. Only seconds later, Brian and Elizabeth would fade into the night. As this is being written, there are other details that we are not at liberty to talk about because of the pending trial.

Mary Katherine is a very strong little girl, but outside of these investigation interviews we realized that she wasn't talking about Elizabeth at all—not even the good times they shared. Mary Katherine was afraid that people wanted to talk to her about the kidnapping all the time, and it frightened her. Lois reassured her that it was okay to talk about Elizabeth without talking about the kidnapping. With a little encouragement, Mary Katherine slowly started bringing Elizabeth's name into conversations. She'd talk about the trips we'd taken, sleeping in the same room, and the sisterly bond they shared. Mary Katherine wanted to focus on the wonderful, happy times we had together as a family, and this helped her tremendously to bring Elizabeth back into our home while she was gone.

By Thursday afternoon, workers from both foundations had several volunteers running the Elizabeth Smart Search Center at the Shriner's Hospital. They brought a copy of the search manual created by the Laura Recovery Center, instructing parents on how to run such an effort. Dawn Davis, a volunteer from the Texas center and the sister of the volunteer who had been first to arrive, flew to Salt Lake City to join the effort. They held a training meeting to direct the searchers on safety and organization of search parties, which was important, because we would later be told that we could be personally liable if someone got hurt while searching for Elizabeth. Within forty-eight hours of setting up the center, help was coming from all over the area. We marveled at the number of people who were there to help—almost 2,000 volunteers. Family had rounded up ward members, extended-family members, and friends, arranging for nearly five times the number of people used in a typical search. Did this give us an advantage? We certainly thought so. If Elizabeth was out there, we would find her and bring her home.

The two foundations' teams did their best to organize the search. They were very helpful.

For the most part, we were unaware of all the details that made up the central command center that was functioning as the Elizabeth Smart Search Center. We stopped by the center as often as we could, but we wanted to stay near the house in case Elizabeth tried to contact us or a ransom was called in. Members from both sides of the family had primary contact with and were part of the search staff. The teams of experts were capable and very dedicated. Many who lived in Salt Lake who wanted to come down and search were given the day off to help. Business owners were incredibly supportive, donating so excessively that we actually had a surplus of items. Donations came in to help pay for the expenses. Volunteers headed into the hills on those hot summer days, instructed to look for anything suspicious and to contact central command with any leads. The search turned up every hair clip left behind on the trails, Band-Aids, bits of cloth, berets, pieces of litter, and even a roll of duct tape. Anything that a young girl might have used—they found it.

For the first forty-eight hours, nothing seemed to turn up that helped bring us closer to finding Elizabeth. Then, around 7:00 P.M. on Thursday, a twenty-two-person search group saw a man wearing a white T-shirt and a white baseball cap. He was pacing back and forth as if he was waiting for something. Someone shouted at the man, sending him scrambling into the thick brush in Pinecrest Canyon. Searchers then heard at least two gunshots. Searchers thought this was a breakthrough in the case. Search dogs were let loose and helicopters were dispatched to fly over the mountains to look for this man. The effort yielded nothing.

At the end of each day, volunteers were debriefed about their searches; a copy of each report went to the police, another was kept at the center, and a third was turned over to us. The importance of and need for trust among local authorities, the federal investigators, and the family was stressed. Hundreds of leads resulted from the search. The police worked around the clock tirelessly. It became apparent that the police, who at one point numbered over a hundred, had become overwhelmed, as the entire situation was intense. There was some concern about the follow-up on leads—some were not followed up on at all, and some were lost. Leaks to the media were also beginning to occur—yet another intrusion on our privacy and a source of mistrust between the police and us.

Chapter 10

Ed

We may pass through the fiery furnace; we may pass through deep waters; but we shall not be consumed nor overwhelmed. We shall emerge from these trials and difficulties better and purer for them if we only trust in God.

—George Q. Cannon

THE INVESTIGATION PROCESS took a tremendous toll on me personally. As we've mentioned before, the procedure in these types of cases is to look closely at immediate family members—no one is above suspicion. All sorts of rumors were floating in the press about our family. The plan police put into action was to exert enormous pressure on family members who might have knowledge about the crime. From that perspective, our case was not exceptional.

After our home was sealed as a crime scene, the police turned the girls' bedroom upside down looking for clues. Had Elizabeth been corresponding with anyone out of the ordinary? Maybe one of the other children was involved in some kind of cult or organization that had an interest in abducting Elizabeth. As outrageous as it seemed to us, statistically the likelihood was that a family member was involved. We, of course, knew that no one in our family was capable of committing such a horrendous crime.

Unfortunately, when the investigators started looking at our family, the obvious thought was that I might be involved. In further questioning at the police station, they kept challenging my honesty and integrity. This was definitely one of the lowest points of my life. I hadn't slept for days after Elizabeth was kidnapped. I was unable to close my eyes without seeing my daughter's image. The police were pushing me to the point of breaking—which was their goal. If they could break me, surely I'd confess. But confess to what? I had done nothing wrong. As if it wasn't enough what Elizabeth's abduction had done to our foundation as a family, the painful effects of all this stress had put me in a state of profound despair.

I was emotionally and physically exhausted, and I was finally at the breaking point. I had been crying uncontrollably for three days—since the morning Elizabeth was taken. That night two FBI agents had to help me up the stairs to my bedroom, since I was unable to make the climb on my own. A little later, around eleven, Lois called my dad and told him she thought I needed help. He came over right away and suggested I get medical attention. The impact of what was happening was settling in, and my mind was overwhelmed by the situation our family was facing. I was checked into the hospital, unable to stop myself from crying.

By morning I had suffered what my doctors would later tell me was a mild nervous breakdown. I was in my deepest despair—feeling totally and completely helpless and unable to save my missing daughter. I was unable to function in any capacity, let alone offer security to Lois and the children. I needed sleep. I wasn't thinking clearly—I wasn't making good decisions. They sedated me when I checked in, but I kept right on crying. I just couldn't stop. I knew more than anything how much Lois and my family meant to me. Regardless of how bad things felt in that moment, I had to get back to my family. I asked for an ecclesiastic blessing. My father came to the hospital with my bishop. The bishop gave me a blessing that I would be able to cope with things and that I would have the strength and wherewithal to get through this nightmare. I had received many blessings in my lifetime, but I was in real pain and in dire need to feel the comfort that only God can give. During my blessing, I felt that God spoke to me. The Lord wanted me to be home with my family. I realized that life wasn't always going to be sweet, but I knew in my heart that everything was going to work out. I got out of the hospital bed, pulled myself together, and went home.

At that point, Lois's strength was the glue that held our family together. Our marriage had always been strong, but after I came home from the hospital, we knew that our connection had to get even better. Between the press outside our door twenty-four hours a day, the invasive line of questioning from the police, and the pressure we were both feeling from Elizabeth's absence, the stress could have torn us apart. We were on the edge all the time. This experience brought out the best and the worst in all of those involved. Lois and I learned how to depend on each other for our individual strengths. When nothing tests you, it's hard to know how you'll react in a time of crisis. Up to this point, we had lived a pretty good and easy life. But the situation in which we found ourselves brought out the differences in our personalities and backgrounds, and we learned what each of us was truly made of, our strengths and our weaknesses.

The searches continued with teams made up of a fascinating cross-mix of the people who make up our city; doctors, students, tourists, construction workers, teachers—everyone seemed to offer some assistance. The one lead we were able to provide was based on what was missing from Elizabeth's bedroom—a description of the red silk pajamas and the running shoes she wore that night. The shoes were size eight, white with blue trim, and with an unusual pattern on the soles.

On Saturday, Lois and I faced the media once again, standing at each other's side. We knew in our hearts that Elizabeth was still alive. My brother Tom spoke on behalf of the family, echoing our belief that Elizabeth was still alive out there. He pleaded for people to check their basements, check their homes. Someone knew something—of that we were certain.

"If you can hear us, we love you, Elizabeth. We haven't forgotten about you. We won't stop until you come home."

Lois choked those words out as she faced the cameras one more time. It was painful to have to make such remarks. Why had we been targeted? We were still so perplexed about the nature of the crime.

At eleven o'clock that morning, police gave out a composite sketch of a man they wanted to talk to who had attended a number of Elizabeth's harp concerts shortly before she disappeared. We had never seen the man they were seeking, nor did his description fit that of anyone we knew. By the afternoon, that lead had proved to be yet another dead end. Police had found the man, but after questioning him, they were convinced he knew nothing about Elizabeth's whereabouts. We were so hopeful that he was the kidnapper. This was just the first of many in a cycle of ups and downs. There would be numerous leads in the months to come that would turn out to be nothing. There was a disfigured body of a young girl found near the Great Salt Lake, bear bones that were discovered outside of Heber, and a desert mound that turned out to be buried garbage. Every time we heard the news of a new clue, our hopes were raised, only to be flattened as each one proved to be unfounded.

Soon after, *America's Most Wanted* aired its first piece on Elizabeth's disappearance. As its name implies, the show highlights unsolved criminal cases, fugitives, and missing children. The show's host, John Walsh, was contacted in an effort to enlist his help and support in Elizabeth's kidnapping case. *America's Most Wanted* camera crews had been around our home since the news first broke, so we were hopeful that John would want to help in any way he could.

Soon after the segment aired, tips started pouring in to the show's phone lines. Walsh reported the latest information from the police that Mary Katherine had feigned sleep during the kidnapping and that the kidnapper didn't know she had seen him. Until just before the airing of *America's Most Wanted* that night, the police and I had publicly indicated that Mary Katherine had been directly threatened by the kidnapper, which was incorrect. John was a great help through the many months of the investigation, and we are very grateful for all he did to help our family bring Elizabeth home.

Chapter 11

LOIS

If the Latter-Day Saints will walk up to their privileges, and exercise faith
in the name of Jesus Christ, and live in the enjoyment of the fullness of the
Holy Ghost constantly day by day, there is nothing on the face of the earth
that they could ask for, that would not be given to them.

—BRIGHAM YOUNG

WHEN ELIZABETH WAS TAKEN, I couldn't see beyond that day. I
truly believed that she'd be home, in her own bed, by nightfall. But
our lives were turned upside down. Our home had been sealed off as
a crime scene, and our children were not allowed to come home. The
children stayed at my mother's for the first several weeks. She has a
wonderful big yard with swing sets and lots of things for the children
to do and lots of cousins for them to play with. I think the whole
situation was confusing for everyone. Our youngest child, William,

didn't comprehend that Elizabeth had been kidnapped. He thought she was having a very long harp lesson. Charles understood the severity of the situation. All the children had suffered a shock to their system in one way or another. While Elizabeth was missing, Mary Katherine prayed that no harm or accident would come to her family. She never once gave up hope for Elizabeth. She collected things she thought Elizabeth would like during the nine months. She'd go to birthday parties and save her goodie bags. She and Elizabeth used to keep scrapbooks together, and Mary Katherine pressed on with that hobby by keeping scrapbooks of letters she received and letters she wrote to Elizabeth. Before Mary Katherine came home from Lois's mother's, we felt it was important to redecorate the girls' bedroom to help Mary Katherine feel more comfortable in that space, since the police had taken most of the bedding and a box full of items from the room. The room was the same, but with a few new items. Mary Katherine always left one side of the room for Elizabeth. She never—not once—took something of Elizabeth's and said, "This is mine now." She asked to borrow something of Elizabeth's as if her big sister were away for the weekend.

My mother was in mourning for her husband. Maybe, in some small way, having the children around was helpful for her, because it took her mind off the situation of Elizabeth being missing and her husband being gone. Meanwhile, Ed and I stayed in our home with Charles and the FBI as investigators searched our home for clues.

As one day stretched into two and then a week, and finally, months and months, my whole attitude changed. A box of Kleenex never seemed big enough to capture all of my tears. Each tissue would just disintegrate. I was able to handle the situation to some degree because of my testimony in Jesus Christ and a loving Heavenly Father. Without that knowledge, I doubt that I would have been able to get up every morning. I hadn't given up hope. There was a chance that Elizabeth was still alive and that we would find her.

For all the obstacles and disappointments we encounter in life, and as painful and difficult as some of our tests of endurance are, they are catalysts to greater understanding. They offer power, peace, comfort, healing, and strength to face the daunting task of climbing a mountain as big as Everest. This is part of life's journey.

The mind is an amazing machine. It can take us to faraway places, shield us from harm, and sometimes even play tricks. When Elizabeth was gone, she was always in our thoughts. Not a single day or minute slipped by without our wondering where our daughter was. Was she safe? Had she eaten? Was she warm? Was she frightened? What was she thinking? What terrible atrocities had she been subjected to? If we had let them, our minds could have wandered to the most terrible and unthinkable scenarios. We chose to put our focus and attention into channeling that negative thought into positive. We did that through daily prayer and reading scripture. Looking back on it, the scriptures we read all took on a new and more powerful meaning. When life is going along smoothly, the ritual of reading scripture doesn't have the same impact as it does when you are in the midst of a crisis. We found ourselves deepening the level of our spirituality. We wanted to search and ponder and pray harder than ever before, and we did just that. We had to do everything within our power to make ourselves worthy of the blessings we were asking for. What good is asking for something and then doing nothing to make it come to pass? Nothing good happens without hard work. You have to do your part.

We visited the Temple the week Elizabeth was kidnapped. We were both exhausted and had no time to let our guard down and decompress. We had been going for days without any sleep. The Temple was the first place where we both felt as if we were protected from the outside pulls of the investigation. The Temple is a place of worship, and it felt so good to be there. We were married in the Temple. It is a very meaningful place to us. For those few hours, life felt normal and we were at peace. The weight had been lifted from our shoulders, though we were painfully conscious that our ordeal was far from over.

Keeping that sense of peace wasn't always as easy as we would have wished during the months Elizabeth was missing. The investigation was intrusive to say the least, but the mess left behind after investigators rummaged through our home was indescribable. We've all seen movies in which a house is dusted for fingerprints. Have you ever given a thought to that becoming a reality in your home? When the police and FBI combed our home inside and out, seeking any clue that might help their investigation, they covered the house in graphite, which is a dark gray—almost black—powderlike substance. How could we bring our children home and make the house look normal when there was graphite everywhere? The carpets needed cleaning, but whom do you call to get graphite stains out? We called our regular carpet-cleaning service, who had cleaned all of the carpets in our home just before Elizabeth was kidnapped. We felt comfortable having this service come into our home—as we've used them many times in the past and trusted the workers to be honest and upstanding. The service was so generous and kind—they came and cleaned the carpets free of charge.

The police came and went for what seemed like days. They urged us to look around for anything that might be missing. If you have teenagers, you will understand when we say we were uncertain about how to look in Elizabeth's bedroom to see if anything was out of place! Two young girls sharing a room doesn't exactly add up to neat shelves, drawers, and closets. As far as we could tell, only her running shoes were missing.

Getting through those first few weeks was critical. All I wanted to do was curl up into a ball and hide under the covers in bed. If I ignored the reality of the situation, I became useless as a mother and wife. My children needed me—and I wanted to be there for them as their mother. After Elizabeth was kidnapped, no one really knew what to say when they'd see me. If I went to the store, there would be so many well-intentioned people who wanted to offer me comfort and condolences. "How are you, Lois?" There was no answer to that. What could I say? I appreciated their efforts. When it was too hard to face going out of the house, I often called on family and friends to run these errands for me.

There were lots of friends who helped in so many ways, but one friend in particular became very important to me while Elizabeth was gone. I believe that she was absolutely guided to help me in the way that she did. It became increasingly difficult for me to function and perform the daily routines of running a home and looking after five children. I don't know how she first heard the news that Elizabeth had been taken, but she found me around ten o'clock that night at Ed's parents. She came up, knocked on the door, walked in, and threw her arms around me and held me. She had the right words at that moment, which offered me some comfort that Elizabeth was being watched over and protected. She had an optimism that helped me cope. She never waited for me to call and ask for help—she somehow instinctively knew what needed to be done. I couldn't tell anyone what I needed. I was numb and unsure myself what needed to be done. It was wonderful to have a friend I could talk to. She was completely removed from the whole situation because she wasn't family, and she could listen without any judgment, regardless of what we talked about. I think that most people simply didn't know the right thing to do—and looking back, I'm not sure there was a right or wrong answer to that.

We believe we were guided and directed in everything that we did during the investigation. There were no coincidences. Everything unfolded in its chosen time. We had switched into survival mode. Our world had stopped when Elizabeth was kidnapped. Everybody was there for us—so when we started to think about Elizabeth, about who was there with her and wiping her tears, it was too much to absorb. I often wondered if I had been crying for Elizabeth or for my own pain. How could I separate the two? Obviously, the tears were for our daughter. We had thousands of people helping us try to get Elizabeth back—and she had no one. We had volunteers hanging posters and donating food, lining up press conferences, and doing anything else they could do in the effort to help. No one was physically there to help Elizabeth or take care of her needs, though I knew our Heavenly Father was aware of her situation.

Praying and reading scripture was a daily practice for us. I also started reading other books that were extremely meaningful and comforting to me. I wanted to understand why this was happening. Ed and I had very different ways of coping. We both wanted the same thing—for Elizabeth to be safe and be returned to our arms—but we dealt with our emotions completely differently. Prayer was the common heart we shared in our coping. We both strongly believed that she was alive and out there somewhere. Regardless of where Elizabeth was, she was in the Lord's hands. If she had been dead, I felt comfort in knowing she was with her Heavenly Father and her grandfather, and that she was in a much better place. I knew that I would see her again, for we are an eternal family.

Let thy heart be of good cheer before my face; and thou shalt bear
record of my name, not only unto the Gentiles, but also unto the Jews;
and thou shalt send forth my word unto the ends of the earth.
—D&C 112:4

Sometimes things happen in life that make us feel as though we are being challenged with more than we can endure. I'm not sure why these things happen, but I believe that bad things do happen to good people. A few weeks after Elizabeth was kidnapped, I was having a particularly bad Sunday. To be honest, there were many, many bad days—but Sundays were especially hard. That is the day that we go to church together as a family. The children had come back to live at the house, and we were trying to get back to a routine. I got all of the children ready for church, but I simply couldn't muster the strength to pull myself together. I was lying on my bed, looking up at the ceiling, feeling lost and distraught. I had been crying and crying. I kept praying in my mind for an answer to why this could be happening. I lay there and said to God, "You have given me more than I can handle." Scripture tells us that God will never give us more than we can handle, but at that particular moment, I totally disagreed. I prayed for God to take away my pain. And then I heard a voice in my head, clear as anything I have ever heard, say the words "Be of good cheer." I couldn't begin to comprehend what that was supposed to mean. I remember thinking, "How could I be of good cheer in a situation like this?" I became intrigued with why those words had been given to me. It was enough to get me out of bed that morning. I dressed and went to church.

Later that day, those very words appeared in the text of a book I was reading, Brent L. Top's *Why Bad Things Happen to Good People*. It was so poignant. I researched scripture that directed good cheer and found two passages in the Bible that refer to these remarkable words: Acts 27:25, "be of good cheer: for I believe God that it shall be even as it was told me," and John 16:33, "these things I've spoken unto you, that in me ye might have peace. In the world, ye shall have tribulation, but be of good cheer; I have overcome the world." God has always sent messages to His disciples to "be of good cheer." Those words were meant to encourage me to live. Elizabeth was His daughter before she was mine. He loved her many times more than I could even comprehend. So, if she was with Him, "be of good cheer." If she were to come back to me, "be of good cheer." Either way, "be of good cheer." It suddenly made so much sense. I had to start living again, because the alternative was unacceptable. I had to trust in the Lord, believe, and be faithful. After that epiphany, life got a little easier.

I never forgot Elizabeth was gone—not even while I tried to stay busy—but I slowly started to realize that I would have to get back to the routine of my everyday life. Whoever stole our daughter was not going to steal my family. I refused to let him or anyone take over my life, and I certainly wasn't going to be filled with anger. A heart consumed with anger has no room for love. I think Ed and I realized early on in the investigation that anger wasn't going to get us anywhere. It would only make things worse. In a way, the fact that I never felt anger was a miracle. Wallowing in anger would have been counterproductive to the investigation, to our family needs, and to ourselves. Instead of feeling angry, I put my attention, energy, and focus on feeling hope and taking care of my family.

Hope, like faith, is the evidence of things not seen. You can't have faith without hope. Hope is like the precursor to faith, and faith becomes the sustaining power. If you give up hope, you give up faith. None of those things are diminished by the outcome of whatever happens in our lives. We will all have adversity. We can either become stronger and better because of it, or weakened because of it. Our faith can be strengthened through our hard times. Some of the strongest people I know are those who have suffered tremendous misfortune in their lives. Those are the people we ought to look to— I have seen what they went through. I have been through it myself, and I believe I have become stronger because of the experience.

We don't always recognize miracles that happen in our lives, but they happen on a regular basis. I believe that miracles are a part of everyone's life. They are as old as the scriptures. I don't believe that Elizabeth's disappearance was a miracle, but I certainly believe that miracles occurred throughout our ordeal and even since she has been home. Our prayers became more intense and more sincere. Our love for one another was greater. Our relationships became stronger. It is a miracle that we were able to live our lives with our daughter missing. It was a miracle that we were strengthened from the experience. It is a miracle that she was able to survive the conditions in which she was forced to live. It is a miracle that she is doing great being home and getting back to life as she knew it before she was taken.

When facing adversity, you face choices. You either get stronger and better, or you weaken and die. We all had our strengths, and we came together as one family to magnify those strengths. Through our collective efforts, we were able to witness the greatest miracle of all—bringing Elizabeth home. But it is important to say that while the outcome was the best possible answer to our prayers, we would have come out of this much stronger and been able to move forward either way. There would have been a terrible void in our lives, but we would never let anyone forget Elizabeth.

When our children returned home, we asked for a blessing on our home that a peaceful feeling would guard against any sense that we could be invaded or violated again. The blessing bestowed on our home remains one of the most comforting and meaningful experiences we had during those difficult months. There was an instant calm surrounding us, and the house was filled with love, safety, and protection. It wasn't a sensation that only we felt. Our electrician would later tell us that he felt a peacefulness at our home. He said that it had a different spirit about it that was calming in an otherwise tumultuous time.

A few weeks later, a window washer came to our home, not knowing who lived there. He had been knocking door to door in the neighborhood, looking for work. When I answered, he said, "Oh, I am so sorry. I didn't realize this was *your* home. I would be most honored to wash your windows free of charge." We didn't feel like it was right not to pay this man for his services. However it also didn't seem like the time to have a stranger do any work around the house. I asked him for an estimate and his phone number and told him that when the time was right, I would call him to do the work. He left his card. We eventually called him, sometime after Elizabeth came home. When he got to the house, he said, "You know. I was so impressed when I came here. I just felt like I was on sacred ground. There was a very special feeling at your home." Despite what had happened, we never felt our home had any evilness in it. Happiness does not stem from wickedness.

Chapter 12

Faith is something greater than ourselves that enables us to do what we said we will do. To press forward when we are tired or hurt or afraid. To keep going when the challenge seems overwhelming and the course is uncertain.

—GORDON B. HINCKLEY

THE SUNDAY AFTER Elizabeth's kidnapping, Ed's sister Cynthia stood in front of the news cameras and said, "The person who has Elizabeth was confused. He cares for her and doesn't know what to do. The solution is to put your feelings aside and send Elizabeth back to where she feels most at home. Let her walk out to a public place where people will recognize her." This request would later become a strange and frightening reality. Our family had been praying that the heart of Elizabeth's abductor(s) would be softened.

Every day during family prayer, each of us would individually pray for the safe return of Elizabeth. Our youngest son, William, wasn't able to pronounce the word *abductor*, so he prayed that the *conductor* would let Elizabeth go. His innocence was a breath of fresh air in this otherwise horrible situation.

The search center had a plethora of volunteers that Sunday morning, who arrived in droves as the day went on. Later that night, five hundred people gathered for a candlelight vigil to pray for Elizabeth as a community at Liberty Park. We drew some comfort from being with those people who came out to show their support of our family. Support was much needed, as Ed had faced yet another test of his word earlier that day. Police had subjected him to an intense four-hour lie detector test. Since we knew he had nothing to hide, he agreed to the test despite his already frazzled state of mind. It was four hours of torture, but the flickering candlelight during Elizabeth's vigil brought a sense of peace to us after a very long, hard day and week. As the sun set behind Liberty Park, Ed offered a prayer for Elizabeth. We could hear weeping coming from the gathered crowd. The love and support we felt was overwhelming.

———————

The Elizabeth Smart Search Center was originally set up at the Shriner's Hospital, but the constant flood of volunteers turned out to be too much for the hospital. Arrangements were made to move the center across the street to the Federal Heights Ward, where it would be held for about a month. Later the center would move to Lois's brother's office, and then again to Ed's brother David's home, where it would reside for the remainder of the search.

Tom, like Ed, had also been considered a suspect, as were Ed's other brothers, David and Chris. Each of the brothers played a crucial role in the search. Tom's polygraph was inconclusive, but eventually he was cleared from suspicion, as were David and Chris. The Smart brothers were offended at being singled out as suspects, yet, interestingly enough, the police never went to the trouble of interviewing their wives to ask for alibis. They methodically questioned male members of both the Smart and Francom families, but only the Smart brothers were subjected to polygraph tests. Were we beginning to feel resentful of the focus on the extended Smart family? Yes. Of course. Absolutely. But, as always, we would have done anything for Elizabeth. If this is what we had to endure to turn the focus on the real perpetrator, we were willing participants.

The next possible break in the case was when police announced they had identified the driver of a strange car that had been seen cruising our neighborhood two days before Elizabeth was kidnapped. Charlie had been our neighborhood milkman for quite some time, so he took note in the early-morning hours of June 3 when he saw an unfamiliar car driving slowly up and down our street. As he passed the car, Charlie waved to the driver in greeting and felt it was strange when the driver didn't reciprocate the gesture. The attitude and actions of the driver made Charlie nervous, because other milkmen had been robbed in the area. As a precaution, he scribbled down the license plate information as best as he could make out. After hearing the news of Elizabeth's disappearance, Charlie called the police to report what he had witnessed two days before the abduction—either a Nissan or a Honda with a driver who was short and wearing a white cap. The plate number he had recorded did not have a match in the Utah database, but the police believed that the first three numbers were nonetheless correct.

At the candlelight vigil for Elizabeth on Sunday night, police almost caught the mysterious driver by chance when people in the crowd complained about a man who was drinking beer and acting strangely. The police failed to reach the man across the crowd before he got away, but they discovered that he drove off in a green, four-door Saturn with plates bearing the assumed correct three digits Charlie had provided. Days later, a little boy found the plate from this car discarded near a baseball field next to a major roadway about fifteen miles from Salt Lake City. The plate, numbered 266-XJH, had been reported stolen. With this evidence, police were able to identify this person as Bret Michael Edmunds. Edmunds had two outstanding warrants and a history of crime. He was wanted on a charge of fraud and for assaulting a police officer. Search dogs even traced his scent into one of the canyons where searches for Elizabeth had been taking place. But Edmunds didn't fit the description Mary Katherine had given of the man who took Elizabeth. The man she described seeing was five feet eight, six inches shorter than Edmunds.

The following Tuesday, Chief Dinse gave a press conference in which he expressed the feeling that the investigation was advancing. Acknowledging that they did not yet have a clear suspect, he added, "We believe that it is possible that we have already talked to or will soon talk to the suspect that is responsible for this crime." They believed the kidnapper was still in the area, and Dinse addressed a warning directly to him, "We are going to get you. And if you've got Elizabeth, you better release her now."

When police released Edmunds's name to the public the next day, they cautioned that he wasn't a suspect but that they merely wanted to bring him in for questioning. By the time the news went public, Edmunds was leaving Utah. Lead after lead came in, and the search became a cross-country manhunt. As the search for Edmunds continued, the police had their eye on yet another suspect, Richard Ricci. We went to sleep that night feeling like there had been some progress in the case.

The next day, we awoke to a horrifying headline in one of our local papers, the *Salt Lake Tribune:* "Police Eye Relatives in Probe." We were horrified and angered to discover that the police again believed the kidnapping had been an inside job. We had been through every test imaginable, and there was no evidence to support the salacious headline. The article pointed the finger at a member of our extended family. It was based on four unnamed sources, all of whom declined to be identified for the article. The article went on to make the claim that the window screen that had been sliced open in our kitchen had been cut from the inside, which suggested that someone had intentionally cut the screen to allow access to the home, misleading the investigation. The idea was to make the crime look like a break-in. It was later determined that Mitchell cut the screen and entered our home through that window—a window investigators believed was too narrow for a man to enter. Ed's brother Chris, who is an average-size man, easily passed through the window when he attempted to prove to investigators that it was possible. The issue of the cut screen remained a point of contention throughout the investigation.

We were certain of one thing: Someone was purposely leaking

information to create these firestorms. Was it the police? Was it an investigator? Why did the *Tribune* have the story when the *Deseret News* didn't have any of the same information? Was a conspiracy brewing?

The day the *Tribune* article ran, our frustration was deepening and Ed's brother David spoke on behalf of the family. David said that we understood the police had a job to do. If they had not investigated the family, they would be remiss in doing their job. However, the time had come to shift that tide. It didn't help that later in the day Chief Dinse said that the police were not eliminating anyone at that point.

Mary Katherine should have been a key element in satisfying police that a family member was not responsible for Elizabeth's kidnapping. If she had recognized someone, she would have spoken up. She had been extremely forthcoming about the details she remembered from that night. We decided to issue a public statement challenging the *Tribune* article. It was highly speculative and was diverting the public focus and attention from the ultimate goal—finding Elizabeth. Lois's brother publicly concurred that the family put no credence in the story.

Shortly after Elizabeth disappeared, Marc Klaas showed up in Salt Lake offering to help us in our plight. Marc had become a public advocate for missing children after his twelve-year-old daughter, Polly, had been abducted from her bedroom and murdered in 1993. He tried to convey to us what we needed to do to move forward—to keep the story in the press. We had been grateful to meet him, knowing he would understand the pain we were in. We wanted to hear what he had been through so we could prepare ourselves and understand what to expect, knowing that the day might come when we'd have to hear the news that Elizabeth was dead. We also understood that we would have to move past that moment, because living for Elizabeth's kidnapping would not allow us or our family to have a life. Fox News also taped a short interview with us.

Though we hadn't originally thought of bringing in a sketch artist to work with Mary Katherine, Marc suggested that we place a call to Jeanne Boylan, a famed forensic sketch artist who had worked on several high-profile cases, including the Oklahoma City bombing. Best known is her hooded portrait of the Unabomber, which helped the FBI identify Ted Kaczynski. She had helped produce a sketch of Polly's kidnapper, and Marc felt she could be extremely helpful to us. He even offered to have Fox News pick up the cost. Unable to reach Boylan directly, we left a message on her machine to call us. But it would later become a controversy in the media that investigators initially chose not to use Boylan, and though we were very interested in having her involved, we decided to back the investigators' decision.

The following week, Tom's daughters, Amanda and Sierra, appeared on *The O'Reilly Factor*, with Marc Klaas also a guest on the show. The Jeanne Boylan issue was raised as the first topic, and our choice to back the investigators was hotly debated. Tom, especially, was strongly criticized. O'Reilly questioned the girls about what they knew regarding the investigation. O'Reilly pushed hard, suggesting that it was strange for the girls to have nothing to add about the details, as "the Smarts are a very close family." At the end of the show, the girls wound up leaving the studio in tears.

Elizabeth's abduction remained a topic on *The O'Reilly Factor* for several days that week (as it was on many cable talk shows), even though there was little new information. It hurt us deeply that our choice to follow the investigators' advice was so roundly criticized and that we were being compared in some places to Susan Smith, who had killed her two young sons a few years earlier.

Chapter 13

BRIAN DAVID MITCHELL had gotten away with kidnapping Elizabeth, but she was never convinced that God was in any way protecting *him*. It seemed as if he was getting away with everything, and he used this to try rationalizing her captivity to her. He paraded her through downtown Salt Lake City without being recognized. She could hear people calling her name in the mountains, but no one ever found them. Would he have killed her if she didn't obey him? Fortunately, this is a question that will forever remain unanswered.

Mitchell and Barzee tried to strip Elizabeth of everything—her identity, her family, her entire person—so that she would no longer be Elizabeth. They even started referring to her as Augustine. Mitchell certainly had a plan in which Elizabeth played a part, and he spoke to her often of how corrupt the world was and how he had been sent to save her from evil. She believed that he would kill her family if she tried to flee or was not cooperative, but she never accepted that he was a messenger of God. People ask us all the time why Elizabeth didn't try to escape—why she didn't try to break free. The answer is simple. She did try, and she couldn't get away. She was never left alone. When the three walked together, Brian and Wanda were on either side of her, holding her hands or otherwise making sure she knew she couldn't run.

When he started bringing her down the canyon, she was forced to wear a robe and veil, which covered her entire face except her eyes. Her face had changed from constant exposure to the sun, wind, and rain. She had grown taller. No one seeing her on the street would have viewed her as a girl in distress, which in itself is remarkable. She went so deep into hiding—for her own safety as well as for ours, she believed. She told us later that she could not live in fear, because to her if she did, her worst fears would come to fruition. She chose to survive. She had no way of knowing whom she could trust.

By trying to destroy everything she connected with her past life, Brian Mitchell thought he could force his beliefs onto Elizabeth until she was, in a sense, reprogrammed. The only other person Elizabeth had contact with in those nine months was Wanda Barzee. Elizabeth was in public many times but never uttered a word. Brian always spoke for her. Many people have asked if Elizabeth suffered from Stockholm syndrome, which is a phenomenon where victims begin to identify with their captors as they fear for their own lives. The personalities of Stockholm syndrome victims do not really disappear and are pretty much the same after the ordeal as they were before. Elizabeth exhibited some of the traits of Stockholm syndrome, but unlike most victims she never bonded with her kidnappers. She did what they said in order to survive. She was never fooled by their diabolical and distorted views. Elizabeth was not the same person physically when she came home—but our daughter still very much existed as we remember her. We believe she did what she had to do to survive.

In Elizabeth's mind, *she chose life over death; life over herself.* She was forced to live a life that wasn't her own. She didn't believe anything her captors said except for the threats of killing her and us. She knew she didn't want to die. She had no way of knowing if there were other people involved. In her mind, Brian had followers watching the house, following our every move. She was led to believe that if she slipped up, we would be harmed. She had to live with that threat every day she was gone.

Elizabeth never left the campsite—her prison—until early August. After her return, people remembered seeing a strangely dressed man and woman with a young girl shrouded in white robes all over Salt Lake. Brian David Mitchell and Wanda Barzee had gotten so brazen and confident they would never be found that they started parading Elizabeth throughout the streets of her hometown. To be sure, there must have been some fear that they'd be caught, since Mitchell insisted she cover her face, leaving only slits for her eyes. They had been in plain sight, but who would have known it was

Elizabeth? The outfit of white robes was mysterious but not strange enough to prompt anyone to question it. We can only guess that people thought that Elizabeth and her captors were part of a religious group.

The hunt for Bret Michael Edmunds ended on June 21 when Edmunds checked himself into a hospital in West Virginia for an apparent drug overdose. He had given a false name when he registered at the hospital, but had used his mother's real phone number as his emergency contact. He was in critical condition, so a hospital worker contacted his family in Utah. A relative called the sheriff's office, igniting a sequence of phone calls between police in Utah and the hospital in West Virginia to confirm that the patient was Edmunds. When the police were certain they had their man, investigators flew to West Virginia to question him. They were able to recover his car, tow it from the hospital, and arrange for a warrant to search it.

We were unaware of Edmunds's arrest until later that day. The news was encouraging, but we didn't want to get our hopes up too high, since Elizabeth had yet to be found. We prayed that Edmunds would cooperate and reveal any information he had about our daughter. The following day, we were hit with our hardest knock from the media to date—make that the tabloid media. The *National Enquirer* came out with a story that sent a crushing jolt through our entire family. At the time, we declined to acknowledge the scandalous report, and we still feel strongly about not commenting. All of the legitimate media covering our story refused to give credence to the story. Many stores in Utah showed their support for our family by pulling the *Enquirer* from its shelves. It was an extremely cruel report that we chose to deal with only after Elizabeth had been returned safely. Five weeks after Elizabeth came home, the *National Enquirer* issued a retraction of its story, admitting it was false and settling an out-of-court agreement with our family.

What became most troublesome to us were not just the articles that were being written, but the continuous leaks that seemed to flow from the Salt Lake Police Department to the media, especially to two reporters working for the *Salt Lake Tribune.* Information was being provided by unnamed sources in law enforcement, and stories were emerging that were filled with accusation, finger-pointing, and bald-faced lies. Further, their indiscretion in selling that information to tabloid newspapers proved to be very damaging to the investigation. There was evidently a need to make news about our family when the story was about our missing child. Why couldn't the focus of the case stay on bringing Elizabeth home?

We could take up several pages in this book lambasting the lack of journalistic integrity of those two *Tribune* reporters, but we have decided, as a family that has endured hurtful and painful lashings in the press, not to put those reporters through what we have been through. These two men have families—wives, children, relatives— all innocent people who would be negatively impacted by the choices those two reporters made throughout the investigation. Enough said.

On the night of July 24, a strangely familiar terror would hit another member of our family. A niece was asleep in bed when she awoke to the sound of picture frames crashing from her windowsill onto the floor. It was a hot summer night and she had gone to bed with her window open. Her family had installed a stop on the window so it could be opened only a few inches. It was open when she went to sleep. She awoke to see an arm poking through the screen. She thought she saw a gun. She sat up in bed, watching in horror as the arm quickly pulled back and disappeared. Her father, Lois's brother-in-law, heard the loud noise and was startled out of bed. He rushed to her room, where he was met by his frantic daughter. He searched the house and found a chair outside the window, propped up against the wall in exactly the same way as was the one that was found outside our home the night Elizabeth was taken. He called the police, who arrived within minutes. Police looked at the window and saw cuts in the screen just like the ones at our home—vertical and horizontal. The police dusted for fingerprints but came up with no solid leads. The police didn't put very much emphasis on the striking similarities of the two break-ins. They stayed at the house for a while but turned up nothing unusual, and after an intense two-week investigation by the FBI, they concluded that the incident was probably a prank by teenage boys. We were not as certain as the police that there was no connection to Elizabeth's kidnapping. It was only after Elizabeth came home that we discovered that Brian David Mitchell had planned to kidnap one of Elizabeth's cousins. He had a list of girls he wanted to kidnap to complete his plan of having seven wives. Brian's mother lives in an adjoining neighborhood as our niece's family. When Brian told Elizabeth that he was familiar with that area, Elizabeth mentioned she had a favorite cousin who lived there. Elizabeth had no way of knowing that Brian was plotting another kidnapping. In the end, Elizabeth hoped and prayed that their dog would be out and scare him away.

The twist to this story is that when the break-in happened, the man police had all but pinned Elizabeth's kidnapping on, Richard Ricci, was sitting in a jail cell. This led us to believe that Ricci may have had an accomplice. Was this a copycat crime, a cruel prank, or was there someone else out there who had kidnapped Elizabeth and was looking to strike again?

The news of the second break-in didn't go public until August 9. It supported our belief that perhaps Ricci hadn't acted alone and that the hunt for Elizabeth had to continue. There had to be someone else who had our daughter, which confirmed our belief that there was a good chance she was still alive. Crucial time was passing, and all eyes were on innocent men. We appreciated everything the police were doing. We supported their efforts one hundred percent. But we know, as the parents of a missing child, that no matter how much is being done to bring your child home, it never feels like enough. Every day without answers was torturous.

In the weeks that followed, we continued to make public pleas to whoever had Elizabeth. We tried to keep the public informed whenever there was news, but we were no longer giving our daily news briefings to the media. Releasing pertinent information was a crucial part of our plan to save Elizabeth. Although the break-in at our relatives' home certainly indicated the possibility of another person being involved, the police felt they had the right man in custody, Richard Ricci. It was hard to ignore the evidence against Ricci, so hard that we couldn't help but begin to believe he was responsible for bringing this terror into our lives. We released a public statement once again asking for someone to please step forward with information about Elizabeth.

To the holder(s) of Elizabeth Ann Smart and Friends Throughout the World: It has been several weeks since our daughter Elizabeth was awakened during the night and taken from her home by force. Every minute of the day we continue to search for her, pray for her, and yearn for her to come home. So many of you have joined us in our search and prayers. Since we last saw Elizabeth on the evening of June 4, we have not received any communication from the person who took her. We continue to eagerly await information about her location. We believe that through awareness of this terrible tragedy in our family many children throughout the world will be saved. As the authorities continue to piece together a puzzle, we still are only interested in one thing—finding Elizabeth. We believe that she is still alive and wants desperately to be returned to us. Whether or not you are the person who took her, we are pleading with you to do the right thing and let her come home.

Anxiously awaiting,

Ed and Lois Smart

After Bret Michael Edmunds was cleared of any involvement in Elizabeth's kidnapping, all eyes focused on Richard Ricci as the primary suspect. When they brought him in for questioning, Ricci, faced with proof, finally admitted stealing Lois's bracelet and to breaking into our neighbors' home but emphatically denied any connection to the kidnapping. The police had checked pawnshops and found one that had a receipt with a detailed description of the bracelet. This allowed them to put on heated pressure to confess to abducting Elizabeth. By admitting his guilt in stealing the bracelet, Ricci had proved to us once again that he was not a man of integrity. He had lied to our faces and he was convincing. The evidence was mounting against Ricci, and investigators seemed to be building a good circumstantial case. Though the police brought him in to be interviewed about the kidnapping, there was no evidence concrete enough to warrant holding him.

Several people were called and questioned by the grand jury investigating Ricci, including his wife, Angela, who steadfastly testified that Ricci was home in bed with her on the night of Elizabeth's abduction. She had given statements to the media on the morning of the kidnapping, expecting that her husband would be fingered. The police administered a polygraph test to Ricci about the kidnapping, which he passed. But he had lied so many times to us. How could we believe him about anything—especially about the disappearance of our daughter?

The biggest hole in Ricci's story revolves around the Jeep we gave him. We were told that on May 30, Ricci picked up his Jeep from Neth's Auto Repair. He returned the Jeep on the morning of June 8. According to Neth Moul, there were approximately 500 to 1,000 new miles on the odometer since he had picked it up. Ricci, who was usually very friendly, was uncharacteristically reserved. He loaded some things from the Jeep into two bags and also took a posthole digger. When he left, he met up with a friend across the street and then disappeared. In the wake of Elizabeth's disappearance, all of this raised several questions in investigators' minds about where Ricci was and what he was doing. It appeared extremely suspicious.

Moul said that on May 30, 2002, he received a phone call from a woman claiming to be Ricci's wife, asking about the Jeep. The story given was that they needed the Jeep to get to work. Neth told them to come and get the car. The Jeep had been ours for two years and Elizabeth had ridden in it numerous times, so any evidence of her found inside would not be enough to implicate Ricci in her kidnapping. Ricci denied he'd taken the Jeep and refused to answer investigators' questions about the added miles. He had several chances to vindicate himself with regard to the kidnapping, but he refused to say where he was, whom he was with, or what he'd been doing. What was he hiding, if anything?

Salt Lake City District Attorney David Yocom filed felony charges against Ricci for theft of money, jewelry, and other items he'd confessed to taking from our home and our neighbors'. In an effort to build a stronger case against Ricci, Yocom also charged him with habitual criminal charges, which, if convicted, would put him in jail for the rest of his life. Ricci was taken into custody, and Salt Lake City police hoped to garner a confession about Elizabeth. They had established that Ricci had a pattern of breaking into occupied homes in the middle of the night. We desperately sought answers— answers we believed Ricci could provide. We wanted Ricci to give us a reasonable explanation for the miles Neth Moul said he'd put on the Jeep. If Ricci wasn't involved in the kidnapping, precious time was slipping away while the investigation was focused on him.

The evidence, even if it was circumstantial, was very convincing. It certainly appeared to everyone involved that Ricci was somehow connected. We wanted truthful answers, and in seeking those, we offered a reward for any information regarding Ricci's whereabouts between May 30 and June 8, 2002. We also offered a reward to any- one who could identify the man waiting for Ricci the night Ricci returned the Jeep to Neth Moul's garage. No one ever stepped for- ward with a single concrete lead in either investigation. Ricci never offered a reasonable explanation about his whereabouts.

In early July 2001, Richard Ricci took part in a bank robbery in Sandy, Utah, getting away with slightly more than seventeen hundred dollars. Ricci was indicted for armed robbery on July 17, 2002. One of the other men involved confessed to the bank robbery, implicating Ricci. This came on the heels of the charges brought against Ricci for the robbery of our home and our neighbor's home. Our understanding was that Ricci was imprisoned and held in a maximum-security facility. Police had hoped that leaving him in solitary confinement would prompt a confession about Elizabeth, but Ricci never admitted to any involvement.

At the roll call hearing in July, Ed pleaded with Ricci's wife, Angela, for the truth. Angela expressed her sincere grief over Elizabeth's disappearance. Ed asked Angela to talk to Richard to see if there was anything he could tell us to help find Elizabeth. He took her by the hand and said, "We have got to find our daughter." He pleaded with her. Angela insisted that Ricci was not involved in the kidnapping but promised to talk to her husband anyway.

But did he take Elizabeth?

The Richard Ricci saga was one of the most difficult aspects of the investigation. The media was obsessed with what we thought about Ricci's case. We didn't want to comment. When we went to the courthouse for the pretrial hearing, there were so many reporters that there was literally no room for us to sit in the courtroom. We were a bit surprised. Someone from the court finally came out and said that only one of us could go inside. We felt it was best for Ed to go, but we were later told that we could both attend the hearing. We had no idea it would be such a big deal. This was just a pretrial hearing. If this was the coverage for the theft charges, we could only imagine the media circus that would follow for a kidnapping trial.

We wanted to sit in on the trial to hear Ricci tell his story, in his own words. Maybe we were looking for a sign that he knew where Elizabeth was—or perhaps we wanted to stare him in the eyes and try to get a read on his alleged innocence. We were seeking the truth—regardless of how upsetting it could have been. There was a motion for a continuance from Ricci's lawyer, who wanted an opportunity for further discovery. What in the world were they looking for? He admitted to taking Lois's jewelry. He stole from us. That was a fact.

After the first day of the hearing, microphones were shoved in our faces by reporters wanting to know how we felt, what we thought, and if were we satisfied with the outcome. Our publicist, Chris Thomas, scurried us through the crowd and told us not to talk to anyone. We were getting used to the crowds, but we never seemed to get comfortable with the attention.

While the investigation into Richard Ricci was still ongoing, we received an e-mail from an anonymous person who claimed to have seen Ricci working on a fence in Wyoming. Somehow, that e-mail got erased. We were just sick over losing that correspondence. We eventually made a public plea to whoever sent the e-mail to resend us the information. We never heard from that person again. We find it hard to believe that any one person can be alone in this world. Someone somewhere knew who sent us that e-mail, just as someone knew whom Richard Ricci met the night he returned the Jeep to Neth Moul's garage. A friend, a neighbor, a family member—someone knew. The Jeep remains a mystery. There was a rumor that someone in Cedar City was able to vindicate Ricci, but we have yet to hear a confirmation of that. Ricci's attorney is bound by client/lawyer privilege, so he cannot reveal Ricci's whereabouts the night Elizabeth was taken.

We never understood why Ricci wouldn't clear his name with respect to the kidnapping allegation. What could be worse than that? And then the unthinkable happened. We received a phone call from Cory Lyman, the lead investigator on Elizabeth's case at the time, informing us that Richard Ricci had suffered an aneurysm in his prison cell and it looked as if he would not make it. Ricci never regained consciousness, and he died on August 30, 2002. The police had placed so much emphasis on Ricci, and there is no faulting their efforts to prove his guilt. They had gone to southern Utah to interview some of his cohorts. They reinterviewed his wife. They did a lot of work, but at the end of the day, it would be all for naught.

School was starting and it was time to resume family life. It was time we faced that Elizabeth might actually be dead. As hard as it was to bear, the thought was becoming difficult to dismiss. We faced that possibility from very different perspectives.

Chapter 14

THAT SEPTEMBER Elizabeth should have been starting her first year of high school—an important milestone for every child. Instead, we had to prepare ourselves for the end of the "summer of missing children" and move forward with the beginning of fall. Whether we were prepared for it or not, this was a new start for all of us. Ricci's death marked a fork in the road for both of us in terms of how we handled the situation going forward.

As painful as it was, we had to get the children ready to go back to school. At this time of year, our daughters were always excited about shopping, while the boys were always indifferent. We feared that the children faced having to answer lots of questions from curious classmates. How were we supposed to prepare our children for the questions we had spent the summer protecting them from? Mary Katherine was of special concern. How would she handle children asking her about being the only witness to her sister's kidnapping? Could their questions be harmful to her memory or her well-being? We sought out expert advice to be certain we had the right answers to these questions. We spoke to the school principals about how to handle the children, especially Mary Katherine. Her principal assured us that the subject of Elizabeth's kidnapping would not be brought up. We can't think of a single incident where a child teased Mary Katherine or made some kind of cruel remark. That in itself was miraculous. She continued to do well in school and socialized very nicely with her friends and teachers. It's amazing how children had more softness in their hearts than did many members of the media. Our other children dealt with the issue as it came up. Andrew goes to the same junior high Elizabeth attended, so the kidnapping came up a little more in his daily conversations than in Mary Katherine's. Charles, being in high school, felt he could handle whatever came his way and never gave anyone a chance to broach the subject. He wanted to be known not as "Elizabeth Smart's brother," but as someone with his own identity. We respected his attitude.

Family became our number-one priority. We both come from such wonderful families, who were there every step of the way to prop us up when necessary. They were a tremendous support system—so many people don't have that to fall back on. We were sincerely blessed to have such a strong sustaining force. It's easy to get wrapped up in life and lose perspective on your priorities and what's really important. Business, bills, everyday life goes on—even when the world feels frozen. We had lost Elizabeth. But life had to go on.

We decided it was important for Ed to go back to work three months from the time Elizabeth had been taken. People helped us out, but it was important, especially for Ed, to take his energy and put it toward something positive outside of the search for Elizabeth. He had been at an emotional standstill, and work provided a welcome break and a familiar sense of normalcy. It was a healthy distraction that helped both of us pick ourselves up and try to go back to the roles we had played before the kidnapping. Work had been a priority for Ed his whole life. The lessons garnered from our experience boiled down to not taking anything for granted. Ed works at home, but he spends a lot of time away from home with clients. Ed's business is one filled with peaks and valleys. When business is good, he's got to capitalize on it so that when things slow down we don't face financial challenges. Ed is an extremely driven man, so when Elizabeth was taken, it was hard for him to function at a level that he was accustomed to. There were numerous distractions that took his time and focus away from his work. Title and mortgage companies, and fellow Realtors, stepped in to help when Ed simply couldn't handle the workload. They made earning a living possible when things became difficult.

For us, Elizabeth's disappearance was a huge wake-up call about life's priorities. Making that one extra deal was no longer as important as getting home to have dinner together as a family. We wanted to be there—to hear how the children's day was, what they did, whom they saw, catching as much of their lives as possible. We held our children a little closer. We told them we loved them all the time. We never expected to hear it back as often as we said it, but the impact on our children was noticeable. They were kinder and more thoughtful to one another. When birthdays came around, they each wanted to do something more special than they had on the last birthday. There has always been a genuine loving feeling in our home, but Elizabeth's absence was a reminder to all of us to be even more peaceful and loving. Life is not all about work and money. Success is not something that is achieved only in the workplace. Life is about living. If you're not out there living it, you're losing out. That point was driven home each and every day Elizabeth was gone. Life is filled with checkpoints that are times to reevaluate how we are doing. We asked ourselves, "Is there anything that we should be changing?"

Lois

I didn't want to believe Elizabeth was dead. I absolutely believed we would one day be reunited—I knew without question that we would see Elizabeth again. I am her mother—I carried this child in my womb next to my heart for nine months. There is no replacing that. How could I ever accept that she was gone—I mean, really gone? I didn't. Not inside. But I knew I still had to be a mother to my five other children. If I wasn't strong for them, I would lose everything I had lived for. I was among the living. I was not dead. I had to endure

the pain and suffering of thinking Elizabeth might be dead—but
not knowing for certain. Equally hard was the thought that she was
living and how horrible things might be for her. Of those two
choices, it was easier to think she was dead and with our Heavenly
Father in a much better place. The maternal instinct defies explanation. If you are a mother, you know what I am talking about. It
comes naturally. It made the hair on my neck stand up when people
would say to me, "I'm going through the same kind of pain." Unless
you've been through this kind of loss, you cannot imagine what it
feels like for a mother to lose a child at the hands of an abductor.
Pain comes in layers, and mine was to the deepest part of my core.
Your pain belongs to you—not your children, not your husband, not
your friends or family. No one else can feel it the way you do. To be
honest, after several months of agony, I didn't want to feel that pain
anymore. It was unbearable to think that someone had my daughter.
Taking care of my family was the only way I could go on.

ED

There was a point when I said to my wife that if she felt so strongly
that Elizabeth was dead, we needed to have a funeral. I was feeling so
incredibly down, and when speaking with John Walsh, as I had done
at times in the prior months, I expressed my need to have a memorial
service. John told me that the likelihood was that she was dead and I
had a wife and five other children to live for. I explained to him how
I couldn't leave her behind; nothing was telling me she was dead. Lois

was vehement that we not have a memorial service (which seemed diametrically opposed to her need to carry on with life), and I couldn't see how I could even come close to moving on until there was one. Throughout the previous months I had been driven and comforted by dreams of Elizabeth walking back into our lives. What incredible elation I felt at those times. It gave me great hope and peace.

Over the months we met other families that had missing children. These families remained traumatized—in many cases for years after the kidnappings. I couldn't imagine life going on like that. I could not tolerate the idea that the monster who took Elizabeth could take us all down—destroy our entire family. I was no longer willing to accept that as a possibility. I don't believe the media always portrayed us that way. Lois is the reason we survived. She is my best friend, and we were in this ordeal together—we would get through it together. There was no way I could have handled this on my own. We are a couple with conviction and devotion to one another, and above all we possess a will of spirit that brings us together. Lois wore a protective coat of armor so that nothing else could get in and hurt our family. She protected her heart, and in the process she protected all of us.

We decided to reveal a key piece of information about the night of the kidnapping. We divulged to the *Deseret News* that a wrought-iron chair that had been moved from our patio had been found by police beneath the kitchen window with the cut screen. This information hadn't been made public before, but we felt it was relevant because it linked the break-in at our niece's home the previous month with Elizabeth's abduction. If no one knew about the chair, how come the break-in had been set up exactly the same way it was at our home the night of Elizabeth's disappearance? With Richard Ricci dead, there were still too many unanswered questions. We wanted to bring as much public pressure as we could to solving those puzzles. We couldn't accept letting the case die with Ricci. We wanted— *needed*—answers.

To some degree, we felt at peace when Ricci died. At the very least, there would be no trial. We would not be forced to relive Elizabeth's nightmare if he was in fact the kidnapper. If he didn't abduct our daughter, what was it that he was hiding right up to the day he died? Who picked Ricci up at Neth Moul's shop? Where did Ricci go from May 28 to June 5? What about those unexplained miles on the Jeep? There had been several sightings of the Jeep in the midwest desert of Utah. Offering a reward for answers, even after Ricci died, had not turned up a single credible lead. We were definitely frustrated.

LOIS

As hard as it was for me to accept, the realization that Elizabeth might be dead continued to set in. It was time to resolve my internal conflict so that I could be a wife and mother to my five other children. In order for this to happen, I had to separate myself from the grueling, sometimes gruesome, daily routine of dealing with the details of the investigation. Our family had already been put through enough in the three months that had gone by. I could see the responsibilities I needed to attend to, I knew I would have to move on to do so, but it took a very long time to even approach the idea that Elizabeth would not be coming home.

We held out hope for her safe return. We prayed, fasted, and looked to God for guidance. This was my daughter. She was the beautiful child whose tears I wiped when she skinned a knee and whose pride I shared every time I heard her play the harp. We had (and still have) a very special mother-daughter bond. That never goes away. Not even in the absence of your child. I would always feel connected to Elizabeth, whether here on earth or in the hereafter. My mind and my heart were dueling over the right thing to do. No one tells you what it's like when you lose a child. I found comfort in reading scripture and other books of inspiration, but mostly I had to come to this decision on my own, and accept that what I was doing was truly the right thing for my family.

Like Elizabeth, I enjoy horseback riding, especially in the mountains above Salt Lake. I enjoy getting on the back of a horse and feeling the open space and fresh, crisp, fall mountain air. It's a time for reflection. On an early-September morning, I drove up to Ed's parents' cabin and decided to ride up the Red Cliffs trail with Ed's father. This was the same trail Elizabeth had ridden so many times before. I hadn't been riding for more than a year. We did most of our riding in the summer. I wanted to go on this ride for Elizabeth. I got her riding boots, her spurs, her riding gloves, and her cowboy hat and wore them on this ride.

At the top of the trail there is a geographical marker that had been placed there several years ago. This place is tied to some very happy moments in my life. We rode our horses to the top of the trail, dismounted, and contemplated the situation our family faced. How were we supposed to move on with our lives? We had no answers. There was no certainty that Ricci had kidnapped Elizabeth. I looked into the valley below and wondered if Elizabeth was somewhere down there. I was weeping. I thought about my role as a wife and mother of our household. It was my role to pick up the pieces of our broken family, but my heart was itself shattered into a million tiny pieces. I grieved every single day, but I had no need to publicly share my torment more than we already had as a family. My way of handling adversity is to do it in the privacy of my own home and heart. For the bulk of the summer, the focus of the investigation and media coverage had been so heavily placed on our family. That added an unexpected pressure to deliver some nugget of information, true or otherwise. It was my opinion that if there was nothing to say, we were better off saying nothing. I didn't feel I needed to be a part of the daily briefings. Everybody wanted to do an interview with the family, but I felt that the less exposure the children had to the media, the less they might realize how big a news item Elizabeth's disappearance had become. I didn't want their lives to be changed more than they already had been.

I was happy that Ed was out there fighting the fight and facing the frenzy. It allowed me to be home. Going to the market was hard. Buying a carton of milk or picking up the dry cleaning meant facing the eyes of wondering friends, strangers, or maybe even Elizabeth's captors, watching, stalking, and planning their next attack. I could feel people staring, wondering what it was like. Wondering how I was doing. Judging. Analyzing. Always reaching out to offer comfort. In a way, Elizabeth became the entire country's daughter, but she was also my daughter. I missed her. I desperately wanted her home. But every night, her bed remained empty.

It was time.

I had to put on a protective coat of armor to safeguard our family—and that coat needed to be big enough to fit all of us inside. I needed to see to it that whoever had taken Elizabeth from us didn't succeed in taking all of us. The situation was incomprehensible. Our family couldn't continue to go through this process of living in the unknown. There were birthdays to celebrate, the start of a new school year was upon us, and there were school plays and recitals to attend. Life was marching on. There is nothing more precious than the bond between a mother and her children. I would never lose that bond with Elizabeth. I wanted to believe with every ounce of my mind, heart, and soul that Elizabeth was still alive and that she'd someday come home. I could not let this destroy our family. Losing Elizabeth had brought us to our knees. The time had come to get back up. I knew what I had to do.

I turned around, took a good look at the panorama of the mountains that surrounded me on the top of the trail, took a deep breath, and began to cry. As difficult as it was to allow my mind to go there, it was time to accept the possibility that Elizabeth was dead.

For Elizabeth to survive, some part of her had to shut down. Our situations paralleled each other quite a bit. Until she left for San Diego, Elizabeth had great hope that she'd be found. She was so close. I had held on to the same hope, thinking that somebody would surely see her. Somebody would recognize her. There were Missing posters everywhere. You couldn't go anywhere in Salt Lake without seeing Elizabeth's face. Ironically, my letting go coincided with Elizabeth's departure from Salt Lake to San Diego. We both changed from that point forward. I had to let go so that my other children could go on. It's not that I didn't want her to come home. It's not that I didn't have strong faith. Of course I wanted her to come home. Naturally I had strong faith. But we were becoming unrecognizable as a family. It was the hardest decision of my life—like Elizabeth, *I chose life over death; life over myself.*

Left: Our wedding day.

Below: Thanksgiving 1986—the Francom family has grown quite a bit since this photo was taken.

Top: The Smart family.

Above: Daddy's little girl . . . a day at the beach with Elizabeth and Charles.

Right: I am so happy. . . . Elizabeth, at eighteen months, sitting on my lap.

Left: Charles, Elizabeth, Andrew, and Mary Katherine hiking at the Indian dwellings in Mesa Verde, Colorado.

Below: Elizabeth and Charles, 1989.

Bottom: Riding horses, one of our favorite activities, at our family ranch in Utah.

Above: Elizabeth and Charles with Nana Avon. Elizabeth had a special bond with her.

Below: Mary Katherine and Elizabeth—our two angels.

Above: Fun in the sun! Edward, Mary Katherine, Elizabeth, and William burying their big brother Andrew in the sand.

Left: Elizabeth and Mary Katherine after their recital, November 2000.

Below: We love Halloween! Edward, Mary Katherine, William, and Elizabeth go trick-or-treating, 2001.

Right: Andrew and Mary Katherine in Hawaii after Elizabeth came home.

Below: We love getting together at Grandma's. She's always up for a good time. Andrew, Grandma Jenny, Charles, and their cousin Myles, 2001.

PLEASE FIND ME

Elizabeth Smart
Victim Description

Age: 14 Years Old	Height: 5' 6" - 168 cm
Gender: Female	Weight: 100 lbs - 45 kg
Hair: Blonde	DOB: Nov. 3, 1987
Eyes: Blue	Missing: June 5, 2002
Clothes: Red Pajamas	From: Salt Lake City, UT USA

Suspect Description
Caucasian Man
30 to 40 Years Old
5' 8" to 5'10"
Dark Hair
Hair on arms and
   back of hands
Light Jacket
Light Golf Hat or
   English Driving hat
Dark shoes

www.elizabethsmart.com

SEARCH CENTER TOLL-FREE 866-FIND LIZ / 866-346-3549
POLICE HOTLINE 801-799-3000

A **$250,000 REWARD** is being offered for the safe return of Elizabeth Smart.
A **$25,000 REWARD** is being offered for anonymous information leading investigators
to Elizabeth or information resulting in a conviction in this case.
Anonymous tip line: **801-799-INFO (4636)**

Left: Elizabeth's Missing poster.

Below: A family photo . . . minus one. Trying to be a family, Christmas 2002.

Above: President George Bush signs the Child Protection Act of 2003, as we look on, in the White House Rose Garden, April 2003.

Right: Elizabeth playing the harp in Washington, D.C., 2003.

Below: Genuine bliss. Our first family vacation after Elizabeth was found. Hawaii, 2003.

Chapter 15

Lead, kindly Light, amid th'encircling gloom, lead Thou me on!
The night is dark, and I am far from home; lead Thou me on!
Keep Thou my feet; I do not ask to see
The distant scene; one step enough for me.

—John Henry Newman

RICHARD RICCI'S DEATH and diminished media attention coincided with the decision to try to move on with our lives. We hadn't given up hope. Lois focused on family and rebuilding our lives, while Ed put his attention toward keeping Elizabeth's name in the media, lobbying for the Amber Alert bill, and keeping the investigation open. He used the one-year anniversary of the September 11 terrorist attacks to draw attention to the importance of security in our homes and our families. He spent more time trying to help get the Child

Protection Act through Congress, a much more comprehensive bill, of which the Amber Alert was only a part. When it became clear that it was going to be harder and take longer to pass the Child Protection Act, we focused on just the Amber Alert. The Child Protection Act would require the FBI to create a national response center to rapidly investigate child abductions. The bill also directs the Justice Department to create a nationwide database of sex offenders that would be posted on the Internet. The bill, if passed, would help to prevent child abductions and would allow potential kidnappers to know the serious ramifications of their crimes. The bill was being heard by the Senate Judiciary Committee in mid-September of 2002 but was unlikely to move forward.

While Lois intentionally started to fade into the background, Ed was ever-present. These roles were fully supported by our respective families. Though our faith was constantly being tested, we remained true to our belief that Elizabeth could still be alive and that if she was, we would find her. By the end of September, our family press conferences were down to once a week. News was scarce.

In early October, we made the first of many trips to Washington, D.C., to meet with President George W. and First Lady Laura Bush. We were there to attend the first-ever White House Conference on Missing, Exploited, and Runaway Children. No explanation was necessary when our eyes met those of the President and First Lady. On our lapels, we wore the buttons with Elizabeth's face. We know the President and Mrs. Bush took notice.

"God bless you both," President Bush said as he held our hands with genuine sincerity.

Then we stood listening to the President address the room. In attendance were Erin Runnion, the mother of Samantha Runnion, who had been abducted from her home in July, and Patty Wetterling, whose son Jacob was abducted at gunpoint in 1989 and has yet to be found. Hundreds of us listened as the President described our plight as every parent's nightmare—a nightmare he said too many Americans are experiencing. It was an infamous group that we didn't want to be a part of but were, sadly, now connected to forever.

The President spoke about a child's life, liberty, and innocence being taken away and what a terrible loss it is for the families as well. To our delight, he said the White House was making the issue of missing and exploited children a priority. For example, the President was urging the House of Representatives to pass the National Amber Alert Network Act—what we had been hoping for since Elizabeth's disappearance. Later that day, we were scheduled to meet with the sponsors of the Amber Alert bill: Senators Dianne Feinstein and Kay Hutchinson and Representatives Martin Frost and Jennifer Dunn. We also met with our local leaders: Senators Orrin Hatch and Bob Bennett and Congressmen Jim Matheson and Chris Cannon. We were so impressed with each of them and couldn't see any excuse for this not to succeed. It was a no brainer: everyone was in favor of it. We needed to send a message to people who prey on children, and this was a good start. President Bush ordered the creation of a national Amber Alert coordinator in the Justice Department, providing for $10 million in funding to implement the system. Although the Senate has passed it almost unanimously in the fall, it had to be reinstated for the new Senate, and in January it was unanimously approved again, 92–0. That our daughter's disappearance made a difference, and that our efforts in Washington had an impact on the passage of the bill, meant for us that we had achieved a small victory over the crime.

In August, in an effort to keep the investigation moving in a forward direction, we wanted to bring a fresh set of eyes to Salt Lake City to look at the evidence and determine if there was something we had all been missing. Henry Lee is a world-famous forensic evidence expert who consulted on the Chandra Levy case, JonBenét Ramsey's murder, and the O. J. Simpson trial. It was hard for us to comprehend that our missing child would now be viewed in the same context as those other high-profile cases. Originally, authorities didn't think it was essential to bring Lee in because the investigation was still focused on Richard Ricci. Investigators eventually agreed to allow Lee to take a look at the evidence, but interestingly, he was sworn to absolute confidentiality with regard to his findings—meaning we were not likely to hear his thoughts or findings about the case. Cory Lyman was an immense help in arranging for Henry to come, but he emphasizzed that Lee had to come at the request of the police department, not at our request. We had been lobbying for Lee, willing to pay for his services out of our own pocket. We were once again out of the loop, though we were hopeful that he could shed light on things and recommend other steps we could take.

When Lee came to our home, he quickly decided that someone could not easily find their way around our house, especially late at night. When Elizabeth was taken, our home was like a fishbowl. We enjoy incredible views from our home. The children had blinds in their rooms, but the house had no other curtains, blinds, or shades.

It would have been simple for anyone to observe the home from the brush that surrounded it. To show how easy it would have been to get into the house, Lee placed a chair outside the kitchen window and showed us why he believed a chair had been a possible method of entry. The chair he used left no marks on the stucco wall of the house when he placed the chair against the house, which seemed to call into question the police's misleading belief that a chair would have made some kind of mark on the wall. Finally, Lee climbed on the chair and demonstrated how far up someone of average height could have cut the screen. Lee appeared certain that a chair and the window were a possible method of entry used by the kidnapper. A forensic study done on the screen had determined that it had been cut from the outside *and* the inside of the house, by a single intruder who had cut vertically down, then reached inside and cut horizontally across to the other cut with a knife, but that information was never released in the investigation.

We went out to dinner with Lee. He told us that he thought the investigators were doing a good job. We derived a lot of comfort from his declaration, but months had passed and the evidence was still inconclusive to the investigators. And why had it taken so long to bring in someone with the skills of Henry Lee? Even after Lee left town, the information he provided would never go public.

Chapter 16

OCTOBER 2002

No matter how serious the trial, how deep the distress, how great the affliction, God will never desert us. He never has, and He never will.

—GEORGE Q. CANNON

I think it might be Immanuel."

It was unbelievable to hear Mary Katherine utter those words. None of our children had seen the man she named for more than a few minutes. We are certain that Mary Katherine received divine inspiration in uttering the name "Immanuel." How on earth could she have come up with his name on her own? We asked Mary Katherine what made her think of Immanuel, and she told us that she'd been reading the *Guinness Book of World Records*. She saw a photo of a very muscular woman, and something triggered her memory of who took her sister the morning of June 5. It's strange, because Brian David Mitchell was a thin man. His pants looked as if they would fall off, so why the name came to her when she was looking at a muscular woman is unclear to us.

Mary Katherine held the secret of who took Elizabeth for a long time, but finally the long-awaited missing piece surfaced. We were adamant about protecting her from feeling any guilt or shame about Elizabeth's kidnapping. She is a hero in so many ways. As the only eyewitness to the crime, Mary Katherine had been unknowingly traumatized more than we can ever imagine. The police questioned her over and over again, but she never wavered from her story. The mind is a mysterious wonder. As a possible method of self-preservation, Mary Katherine blocked out what she had witnessed.

When Mary Katherine came forward with her identification of Brian David Mitchell, it was incredible to us that she had come up with his name, Immanuel,* especially given her very brief exposure to him. But she always contended that Richard Ricci was not the kidnapper. "Immanuel" was the only person she ever singled out. As the sole eyewitness, her coming forward with a name—any name—ought to have held some weight with the investigators, but because she was not absolutely certain, they didn't take her identification very seriously.

Mary Katherine was interviewed yet again at the Children's Justice Center, a place that became all too familiar to our family.

---

* It was first thought that "Immanuel" was spelled "Emmanuel." We discovered that Brian David Mitchell used the "Immanuel" spelling.

After hours of questioning her, the police agreed to try and track Brian David Mitchell at various homeless shelters around Salt Lake to bring him in for questioning. Since it was not his given name, when they put the name "Emmanuel" into the police database, not surprisingly, it turned up no matches. Brian David Mitchell's police record had failed to appear because of a misspelling of his name—"Emmanuel" as opposed to "Immanuel." We never expected that the name "Immanuel" would turn up a clue, because we knew it was an alias. What we needed was his real name. Once I asked Cory Lyman, who took over as head of the task force from Don Bell, when we were going out with the story of Immanuel. He told me, "Probably never. What do we have to go on? An alias name? Three sketches from members of your family that don't look alike. And Mary Katherine isn't absolutely sure." Nothing supported the notion that Brian David Mitchell was the right man. The police remained focused on Richard Ricci as the kidnapper. It was so unlikely that Brian David Mitchell, who had been to our house only one time, for a few hours, could possibly have known the layout of the house well enough to pull off such a crime. Statistically speaking, he was right.

Looking back on it now, we know that much of the description that Mary Katherine had given up to that point was wrong: the clothing, the cap, the beard. It was so astonishing that she'd come up with the name, but the police didn't put much credence in her identification. The man who came to our home was clean-cut, well-groomed, and clean-shaven. Could Mary Katherine have subconsciously been describing the man Lois met on the street because she recognized the voice? When Mary Katherine uttered the name

"Immanuel," everything changed. The case had to be rethought. It was yet another turning point.

Don Bell's assumption that Ricci was 99.9 percent guilty divided the police and law-enforcement agencies working on the case. It seemed as if half of the investigators supported Bell's theory that it was Ricci and half thought it was possible that someone else may have taken Elizabeth.

Every turning point in the case was very much a gift. Each one unfolded this journey in a time frame that, although excruciating and nightmarishly long, had it changed at any one of the seminal moments, we cannot be certain that Elizabeth would be home today. Richard Ricci's death was the biggest defining moment for both of us. That is when Lois decided that her attention needed to be focused on our other children, and Ed, feeling unsettled and without resolution, decided he could not give up his search. Looking back, we know we both could have taken on either role. It just happened that the roles we took on answered the needs of our family.

We had been dragged down about as far as we thought we could go. In life, you can't move on if you are in a deep emotional hole. In our minds, it was in God's hands. We never wanted to think about Ricci again. The police had tried to convince us that Ricci took the secret of Elizabeth's whereabouts to his grave and had encouraged us to accept that he was the perpetrator and try to get on with our lives. Time and time again, we were told by law-enforcement officials that Elizabeth was dead.

When the notion of "Immanuel" came up, it opened our hearts and our minds to a possible light at the end of the tunnel. Beginning to identify Brian David Mitchell gave credence to the idea that perhaps everyone was wrong about Ricci, and that meant having to go back to square one.

We were cautious to withhold this new information from the media until we were absolutely certain that there was some validity to what Mary Katherine said. The police learned that the Church of Jesus Christ of Latter-Day Saints security center had several photographs of a man who went by the name "Immanuel" who had been a nuisance at Temple Square. When we looked at the photos, we didn't recognize anyone. The police then showed the photos to our sons Charles and Andrew at their schools and asked them if they could identify anyone in the photos. The boys couldn't. Lois had absolutely no recollection of what Brian looked like, so she could offer no assistance in the process. We were looking at a long-haired vagabond, not the clean-shaven Immanuel we remembered.

The police then suggested that we work with a forensic artist to help us come up with a sketch. They had brought in a forensic artist to work with our sons Andrew and Charles, but when we saw those renderings, Ed didn't think they looked anything like the man he recalled in his mind. Andrew's looked too young, and Charles told us that he wasn't getting anywhere and quit. We were baffled as to why the police didn't want Ed to give his input; he was the one who had spent three hours on the roof with Brian David Mitchell. He spent more time with Mitchell than anyone else in our family had. It made no sense and added to our frustrations. Ed initially had a vivid recall of what Brian David Mitchell looked like, but as time passed, he feared that he would not be able to help create a strong likeness. One day, in frustration, Ed called Cory Lyman and asked, "Why don't you have me work with an artist?" That morning, artist Dalene

Nelson from Moab had walked into the Salt Lake City police station looking for work, although she did not have forensic experience. She spoke to Cory Lyman, and he decided to have her work with Ed for a day. They worked together for a few hours before Ed had to leave for a business appointment.

When the question arose of bringing Mary Katherine into the process, we decided it was more important to protect her. It made no sense that she came up with the name after looking at a large woman, and Lois didn't want to subject Mary Katherine to anything that would harm her if she was wrong about the name. Mary Katherine had already been through the pressure of trying to identify the kidnapper by working with Jeanne Boylan in August. Their efforts were admirable but did not produce a sketch we could use. It was such a long shot, we weren't willing to sacrifice her for this. The children had made progress getting back into a more normal cycle of life. They were back in school. They were sleeping in their own beds. We were unwilling to take a chance of upsetting the routine we were falling back into.

Ed was frustrated that he and Dalene didn't get as far as he'd hoped. The sketch wasn't totally accurate, but he felt they would get there if he had more time. Dalene was leaving for Moab and wouldn't be back in Salt Lake for at least another week. That was eating away at Ed as he drove to his appointment. He couldn't wait another week. Ed called Cory Lyman, the lead investigator, from the road and told him that we'd pay to keep Dalene in Salt Lake City until she could finish. We'd put her up in a hotel and do whatever it took to finish that drawing. It was an important piece of evidence. So much was riding on getting it finished.

Dalene agreed to stay. She slept at a friend's home that night and came up to the house the next morning. Ed and Dalene worked several more hours, and though the sketch wasn't perfect, it somewhat captured the man we were now looking for. We thought the investigation had all but died, but this new lead encouraged police to take the composite to several homeless shelters around Salt Lake, hoping that someone would recognize the man. Even though Brian David Mitchell eventually turned out to be someone many people in Salt Lake knew, most everyone knew him with long hair and a beard. We had met him looking very clean-cut, so our drawing didn't show a man anyone else could easily identify, which meant our search was once again coming up empty-handed.

As Utah's 2002 hunting season was about to open, we made an appeal to the thousands of hunters to keep their eyes open for Elizabeth or any signs of her. We and some family members attended a press conference and handed out printed fliers with photos of Elizabeth and pleaded with the hunters to take note of anything unusual. We urged them to be watchful, call out Elizabeth's name, do whatever they could to help our family.

Four or five weeks had passed since we had first told the police about Brian David Mitchell. We called and asked what was happening all the time, and they assured us that they were doing all they could. The investigators continued to circulate the sketch to some of the homeless shelters around Salt Lake. The decision to not go public with this information was frustrating at first, and neither one of us fully understood why the police were hesitating. They believed that the allegation was speculative at best—there was no evidence pointing to Mitchell. They had an eyewitness in whom they placed very little faith. They told us they were afraid to release the information for fear of scaring him away. Time was passing, and it felt as if nothing was coming from the sketch that had, until this point, been quietly circulating. It felt as if there was very little we could do to once again make Elizabeth's kidnapping a priority for the police.

There were so many times we wanted to believe that Elizabeth was near, and every one of those leads ended with a roadblock. The thought that we would have to go through this emotional roller coaster yet again was becoming too hard to bear. Every time we heard about human bones that were found in the desert, or sacrificial cultists from all over the world, or body parts in the foothills, or some psychic with a vision of where Elizabeth was, we held our breath, hoping it would not be our daughter. It became all-consuming and made it impossible to move forward. We were stuck between living and dying.

We faced numerous challenges when Elizabeth was kidnapped. One of our biggest obstacles was that we simply did not know how to deal with the investigation and the investigators. We weren't faced merely with the challenge of losing our daughter. We were challenged daily by the media, the police department, the investigation, and the abundance of theories. Ricci did it. The father was involved. Elizabeth was a runaway. None of it was right, none of it helped find Elizabeth. Any one of those theories could have beaten us down, but they didn't. We are not pointing fingers at anyone. Everyone involved in the case and the investigation had a job to do. To this day, there are skeptics questioning what really happened. Those are the same people who question the notion of faith and the power of prayer, which is what we are really trying to get to. It would be a mistake for us to write a book that paints a picture that Elizabeth magically came home without any challenges, trials, or tribulations. We faced them on a daily basis. We supported every effort that was being made to bring our daughter home.

We didn't release Brian David Mitchell's sketch for several months. That turned out to be a blessing. When Mary Katherine stepped forward with the name, it was coincidentally around the same time Brian David Mitchell and Wanda Barzee had fled Salt Lake City for San Diego. If the sketch had come out in October, they might not have ever returned to Salt Lake. Was it divine intervention? We'd like to think so. We believe that this was in the Lord's hands.

Chapter 17

NOVEMBER 3, 2002
ELIZABETH'S FIFTEENTH BIRTHDAY

THERE WAS NO WAY to truly celebrate Elizabeth's birthday with her missing. The only way we could cope with her absence was to try and observe her birthday in a way we knew she would have loved. We took the children on a trip to Disneyland, one of Elizabeth's favorite places. We were supposed to be in California to do Larry King's show anyway, so we decided to make it a family trip. Normally the Magic Kingdom would have been just what we needed; without

Elizabeth it was a bit somber, though we did manage to have some fun. We went on every ride that Elizabeth would have loved. She loved all roller coasters. If the ride was fast and twirled, she loved it. People there stopped us to say hello, tell us that they were praying for Elizabeth, and to keep the faith. We also took the children to Knott's Berry Farm. We tried to have a fun-filled few days before we had to face the cameras and head back to Utah.

The world is filled with good people. Wherever we went, people reached out to us. They wanted to let us know we were not alone. We were accessible, because we're just regular people. Once, on a trip to St. Louis, a woman started up a conversation with Lois. For some reason, she asked where we were from. Lois told her we were from Salt Lake City. The woman talked about her sister who lived in a town in Utah. She proceeded to say that her brother, who lived with her, was getting a divorce and she felt so bad because she never got to see her sister's kids and that she didn't have any children of her own. The woman suddenly turned to Lois and said, "I don't even know why I am telling you all of this. I don't even know you."

"Oh, you might. I am the mother of Elizabeth Smart."

She said, "I thought you looked familiar."

The woman reached out and hugged Lois as tears rolled down her cheeks. She felt terrible for unloading her story. "After everything you've been through, my troubles seem so insignificant."

But her troubles were not insignificant. They were clearly weighing this woman down. Someone's molehill is another person's mountain. Elizabeth's disappearance gave everyone a little perspective on life. No problem feels insurmountable to us these days. We know without question that we can get through anything.

Thanksgiving was especially hard. We went to Lois's Mom's, and there were two empty seats that year—Lois's dad's and Elizabeth's. We didn't physically set two empty places at the table, but the absence was felt nonetheless. Thanksgiving is a time for reflection and giving thanks for all of the goodness we have in life. Even though we had been struggling through the toughest six months of our lives, we still had much to be thankful for. We had a missing child, and yet we still felt blessed. We were thankful for each other and thankful for our families. We had so many people helping us and reaching out to us. People were supporting us from all around the world. It was life-sustaining. How could we *not* be thankful? When we talked to the children about what was in their prayers this holiday season, one of them said they were praying for warm weather so Elizabeth wouldn't be cold. The children never let Elizabeth out of their thoughts or prayers, especially as the holidays approached. Holidays are meant for families. The holiday season has always represented a time of great joy in our family. This year, the holidays were not joyous in the same way they had been in the past. There was a gaping hole in our family, and an even bigger hole in our hearts. We tried to put on a smile.

At the beginning of the holiday season, Elizabeth and Mary Katherine would always participate in the annual harp concert that takes place in November. This year it was held at Utah's Capitol Rotunda. It was dedicated to missing children, with a special tribute to Elizabeth: One hundred harpists, age five and up, tied light blue ribbons on their harps in her honor. Mary Katherine had always been a part of this recital, and this year it was especially poignant because she played Elizabeth's harp. In a way, it felt as if Elizabeth were there with her. At the end of the concert, a medley of songs was played in sync with a montage of photographs of Elizabeth spending time with her family, riding horses, and playing the harp. We were both fighting back tears and feeling the loss more than ever. The end of the concert was perfectly choreographed, with video footage of Elizabeth bowing along with the hundred harpists in the room. Elizabeth's teacher, ShruDeLi Ownbey, her friends, and other harpists from all over Salt Lake had organized this concert to honor her. One of the pieces was a spiritual medley that included selections, played by Elizabeth's peers, called "Motherless Child" and "Wayfaring Stranger." It was very emotional. In our minds, some pieces performed that night belong to Elizabeth. They were signature pieces that Elizabeth often played. Over the nine months Elizabeth was missing, whenever we would hear harpists play those pieces, it was unbearable. Tears flowed down every cheek in the room. We were sobbing throughout the entire concert. It was a bittersweet moment—she should have been there. In a sense, she was, yet she wasn't. The ensemble was playing for everyone in the room, but we felt a special connection, a humbling experience, that those harpists had come together and were playing for us—and Elizabeth, our missing angel. Oh, how much we wished she were there.

Just before Christmas, we flew to New York for a taping of *The John Walsh Show*. John was doing a show that featured the parents of missing children. After the show, Ed took John aside and asked if he could talk to him in confidence. John assured him that he could. Lois and Chris Thomas stood in the hallway with Ed and John as Ed explained that Mary Katherine had come up with a name of the man she believed took Elizabeth. He said that we had a composite sketch but the police were hesitant to make it public. John expressed his concern over the reasons the police had given us for not circulating it. His suggestion was to just come out with it. John Walsh is not the kind of man who holds anything back, and he offered to do another show featuring the new lead information. He could not have been more supportive, though his advice was the exact opposite of that the police had been giving us. When we left, we felt very positive about sharing the news with John. He assured us that he would do the right thing with the information. We headed back to Salt Lake to get ready for Christmas.

Christmas was the hardest holiday. Elizabeth was supposed to be home by Christmas. Somehow we had truly believed our nightmare would be over by then. We couldn't get caught up in the usual Christmas spirit. It felt like it had to be a quiet Christmas. That was hard for our younger children to understand, but the older children understood what was going on. Going to the department stores and selecting games and toys didn't feel right. It wasn't a priority for any of us. In the past, Christmas in our home had been about fun, gifts, and festivity. This year, we got back to the true meaning and spirit of the holiday—the birth of our Lord and Savior Jesus Christ. As a way of honoring their missing sister, each of the children wrote a short note to her as a Christmas wish. Here's what they said:

Dear Elizabeth:

I miss you so much. I can't express how horrible I feel about this. This experience has changed my life forever but I can't even begin to imagine how much it has changed your life. You mean everything to me. You were the perfect sister always trying to do good for everyone. I always imagined you growing up to be this very accomplished person who had gone to the best music school and raised a wonderful family. You were definitely on your way to fulfilling your dreams by the way you always had good grades and tried your best in everything. I just want you to wake me up one morning to go help catch horses on the ranch and for this to all be in the past.

Love,

Charles

Dear Elizabeth:

I wish with all my might that you were here. You are the greatest sister in the world. I wish you were at Disneyland and Knottsberry Farm. You are the best at basketball, snowmobiling, and so fun to ski with. I love you Elizabeth.

Love,

Andrew

Dear Elizabeth:

I miss you so much. I wish you were here to celebrate your birthday with us. Elizabeth, you're the best sister I could ever have in the whole world. I love you so much. I don't want you to get hurt at all. Elizabeth, I miss you playing games with me, the harp, reading to me, and sleeping with me.

Love,

Mary Katherine

Dear Elizabeth:

I miss you so much. I wish you were back home with us. I miss hearing you play the harp and biking to grandmas. I love you so much.

Love,

Edward

I love you Elizabeth . . .
William

The Festival of Trees is a local Christmas event that raises money for the Primary Children's Hospital, a hospital that provides services for people who can't afford them. Every year people donate beautifully decorated trees to the hospital, which the hospital in turn sells to raise money. Some of Elizabeth's close friends and their mothers asked us if they could donate a tree in her honor, and we were very moved by the gesture. These friends decorated a beautiful tree with white angels that each girl had embroidered her own name on, silver harps, and blue ribbons. They decorated a small replica of Elizabeth's tree and brought it to our home. We used that tree as our only Christmas tree that year. We were so appreciative of their sincere thoughtfulness. Some of Elizabeth's harp friends also donated a tree. We went to tour the Festival of Trees and were moved by yet a third tree in Elizabeth's honor donated anonymously. We cried as we walked through the South Town Expo in Sandy. People all around knew who we were and were so kind with words of love and support. We truly felt the Christmas spirit of goodwill toward men. Anonymous friends had made sure that each of our children were remembered by dropping several gifts off on Christmas Eve for their surprise and delight on Christmas morning.

Instead of gifts for Christmas, we decided to give each of the children Christmas Boxes. The idea came from a story Lois read when she was a child. It was the story of an empty box. When the child in the story opens the box, he wonders why it is empty. He is told that the box isn't empty. It is filled with a gift he can't see or taste but he can feel—it is love. We filled five boxes for each child with items we thought were meaningful. Photos of each child as a baby, of them growing up, of the entire family, and photos of Elizabeth. We also enclosed a note in each box telling our children how much we loved them. As hard as it was for the children to not celebrate Christmas as we always had in the past, they loved receiving their boxes. Edward, our eight-year-old, even after receiving other holiday gifts, came to us on the night of Christmas and said that his box of love was his favorite gift.

Here's the letter that went to each of our children in their Christmas Boxes of Love:

Dear Children:

2002 has been a year which we could never have anticipated. Trials of heartache, growth and a test of our faith pushed us beyond anything we have experienced in this life. Life will never be the same. We have learned how precious life is and how important each of you are in our lives. The most precious gift in life is represented in this box. It is not something that you can see, smell, or eat. It will not wear out or decay with time. It will not be forgotten and is not tangible (physical). It has been shared with us by our Heavenly Father and His son our brother Jesus Christ. That gift is LOVE. He demonstrated and shared this time and time again by:

1. *His willingness to serve each of us in fulfilling our Heavenly Father's Plan*
2. *His willingness to atone for our sins*
3. *His willingness to be an example of righteousness showing us the path, which will lead us into eternity where we can be united as a family.*

Each of you, Charles, Elizabeth, Andrew, Mary Katherine, Edward and William, have been sent and entrusted to us. How different our lives would have been without you. There isn't anything in this life more precious.

As we have cried, grieved inside and pleaded for Elizabeth's return, we have remem-
bered those differences that make us each individuals and made Elizabeth what she
is. It pains us to have her gone and we look forward to being together once again.
As we love each of you as parents our Heavenly Father loves us more than we can
comprehend. We have learned that the way we live makes the difference of whether
we will be together eternally. We hope this Christmas will always be remembered
not only as one that Elizabeth is missing from, but one that so much love and
support has been shown to us. Please know that you are most important in our
lives and that in the eternal perspective nothing can be more important than love.

> *Love,*
> *Mom and Dad*
> *Christmas, 2002*

For Christmas we normally travel to Palm Springs, where Ed's family has a condo. We thought it would be a good idea to stick to tradition for the children, so we left the day after Christmas. It is a time when we swim, hike, and horseback ride. We do an annual hike up one of the local mountains, which has turned into a contest between the children to see who can get up the trail first. It's a rough trail. It's rocky, slippery, and usually hot. Elizabeth was always the one leading the pack. One of Elizabeth's best friends, who also has a home in Palm Springs, decided to come on the hike with us. Her name is also Elizabeth—they are a month apart in age. We were so happy to have this Elizabeth with us, but it was a bittersweet reminder of what was really missing.

Our Elizabeth has a tight circle of friends. It was very hard to lose the presence of those girls in our lives. They lost a friend as we lost a daughter and sister. They came around from time to time to see how we were doing, to bring us cookies, and notes and cards of encouragement.

Just before the end of the year, John Walsh appeared on *Larry King* and announced, unbeknownst to us, that there had been a break in the Elizabeth Smart case. Walsh went public with the news of Immanuel. At the time, we were shocked that he had shared this information so quickly and without our knowing that he planned to do so. In hindsight, it was a blessing. It set us on the course that would ultimately bring Elizabeth home.

Chapter 18

IN MID-AUGUST, we received our first ransom letter. It was post-marked from Charlotte, South Carolina. The letter stated, "I have your daughter. Don't try to contact anyone. Don't try to trace this. You won't be able to find me. I'll contact you again in the future." It seemed so far-fetched, but we handed the letter over to the police.

From mid-October until November 4, the day after Elizabeth's fifteenth birthday, the same man claiming to be Elizabeth's kidnapper emerged again, this time on the Internet, asking for a $3 million ransom for Elizabeth's safe return. He was using the screen name of "elizabethsmartkidnapper." The man said either he got the money or he would harm Elizabeth. We had been the recipients of many hoax letters, but we always checked them out just to be certain they were not real. News of someone in an online chat room claiming to be Elizabeth's kidnapper surfaced. The Internet was an ugly place to read about our daughter. There were people with nothing better to do than talk about us: our family—that we were hiding something. It was brutal. It made us so sick to hear what some people were thinking about us, our case, and our daughter. While the majority of the communications we received from around the world were filled with loving thoughts, prayers, and hopes for the safe return of Elizabeth, one bad letter would set us back for days. If there wasn't a return address on the letter or card, we learned, it was usually not a favorable letter and we didn't open it.

In an effort to trap the man e-mailing us for ransom, FBI investigators engaged the perpetrator in Internet communication, pretending they were Ed. They were certain this was not Elizabeth's kidnapper because he was unable to answer important detailed questions about the case. The threats were still a very serious crime, and we intended to bring this man to justice for attempting to extort money from us while we were trying to find our daughter. The investigators were able to determine his physical location through his Web server. The e-mails were traced to South Carolina, being sent by Walter K. Holloway, who was nineteen years old. It honestly made us sick to see this young man ruin his life over a hurtful moneymaking scheme. He will spend a good part of his young life behind bars, and for what?

People came out of the woodwork to extort money from us. Bounty hunters, psychics, religious leaders—you name it, we heard from all of them. If we could simply pay their way to Salt Lake, or if we could find it in our hearts to make a small donation to their organization, or the police aren't doing their job, I'll find Elizabeth—if you pay me! It became ridiculous, but we always had to follow through by speaking to and listening to these people just in case one of them had some bona fide information. One time a man showed up at our house complaining about what a terrible job the police were doing in the investigation. He told us that he was the only person out there really working. He was associated with a group called Soul Miners. He sent us letters all the time with the numbers "671" on the envelopes. We had no idea what the numbers meant. He was very clear that the numbers were on a dollhouse in Elizabeth's room. We assured him he was wrong, but the man refused to leave our house until he saw the dollhouse. Sometime after that, he apparently went to the mayor and told him we had Elizabeth sealed up in a wall, and the police actually came out to our house to question us about his claim! The police diligently followed up on *those* leads— they combed our neighborhood, checking neighbors' homes to see if there was any shred of truth to his story. Finally, one day Ed received a phone call from the same man, claiming he knew who had Elizabeth. He was asking to come right over to the house with Detective Parks. Ed hesitated, telling the man that Lois wasn't home, then hung up and immediately called Detective Parks, who explained to Ed that this guy was a total nutcase. The police had been dealing with him for months. Finally, realizing the guy was trying to get a confession from us, Ed called him back and said, "I don't appreciate what you're doing. I've called Detective Parks, and he knows nothing about your claim. It's horrendous enough that we're going through this, but what you're doing to us is unbelievable. If you call me or come on my property again, I am going to call the police and have you arrested!"

We continued to get letters from him—mostly with pleas for us to come clean and admit what we had done. He warned us that Jesus wouldn't hold us blameless if we didn't repent for our crime.

Even after Elizabeth came home, the strange visits didn't end. A man showed up on our doorstep sometime after we returned from a trip we took to Hawaii just after Elizabeth was found. A neighbor told us that someone claiming to be an old friend had been by the house that morning. He waited around the street until we came home that afternoon. The man finally came to the door. Ed answered.

"Hi, Ed. I'm here. It's me. Val. How are you?"

Ed was clueless about who this man was.

"I helped in the search. You know me, Ed. Don't you recognize me?"

Ed responded, "No. I'm sorry. I don't recognize you. I can't invite you into my house, I'm sorry."

"Well, Lois knows me. Go ask her."

Elizabeth was in the living room playing her harp.

Lois didn't know who the man was either.

Ed went back to the doorway and said, "Help me out here. My memory isn't what it used to be. How do we know you?"

The stranger went on and on about how he was with Elizabeth throughout her captivity. He was in the mountains and was responsible for finding her. Of course, then he told us that he wasn't *physi-*

cally in the mountains with Elizabeth—he was *mentally* there with her. We had heard enough, and we asked this man to leave immediately. We called the police, who warned the man that if he stepped on our property again, he'd be arrested for trespassing. Out of curiosity, we called Detective Parks to ask him if he knew anything about this guy.

"Actually, he was at the DA's office all morning, being a nuisance."

We wondered if the police had done a background check after he'd been in the station. We were told they had not. The next afternoon, we received a troubling phone call from Detective Parks: "Ed, if that guy ever shows up to your place again, call us immediately. He has just been released from prison for kidnapping and assault."

Lois and I reopened our conversations about moving after that call. It seemed that we had no privacy. Everyone knew where we lived, and the threat of one of our other children being taken was very real. The children had just started going places on their own, and once again we had to confine them to the house or insist that they go out with one of us.

Throughout the investigation, it seemed that we would just get through dealing with one crazy person when another would appear. Over and over again, people would show up with their own agenda. Some offered to help us find Elizabeth—making promises of information leading to the capture of her abductors. We had been through so many ups and downs. Sometimes, well-meaning people offered us a little comic relief, though we are certain their intention was to offer comfort and peace.

Chapter 19

*A*s the weeks and months slipped by, life was getting somewhat back to a routine. The volunteers weren't as plentiful, but the searches continued. People needed to get back to work. They had to go back to their families. They had to continue living, even if it felt as if we were slowly dying on the inside. Lois remembers driving in her car one day and wondering what it would be like to look inside the homes she was passing. She wanted to observe these families, these strangers, in their homes. Were they happy? Did they appreciate what they had? She wanted to see how they celebrated holidays—if for no other reason than to see how the real world was living and to get out of her dark place. We were those people once—quietly living our lives in the privacy of our home. Now we were front-page news. The walls of our home were taken down for the world to observe. Our pain, our sorrow, our loss—exposed for everyone to see. As she passed more houses that day, she saw posters of Elizabeth in many of the windows. The blue ribbons that had gone up so quickly after Elizabeth was taken remained all over town. They were on car antennas, fences, trees, and lampposts; harpists all over the country tied them to their harps. Who were all these people who still cared enough for our daughter that they placed a Missing poster in their window, their car, their storefront? Many people continued to wear the pins with Elizabeth's image. In Washington, there were many members of the Senate and Congress who always advocated for what we were doing for other children and what we were going through, including Dianne Feinstein, Kay Hutchison, Orrin Hatch, Bob Bennett, Jennifer Dunn, Martin Frost, Jim Matheson, and Chris Cannon.

Before Mary Katherine said the name "Immanuel," Elizabeth, Brian, and Wanda were probably already on their way to San Diego. Elizabeth has revealed to us that boarding the Greyhound bus in Salt Lake was terrifying because she feared never coming back to Salt Lake and never again seeing her family. That was a huge turning point in Elizabeth's journey. There had been searches in states surrounding Utah, Nevada, Arizona, Nebraska, and Colorado. By the time they left for California, Elizabeth had become resigned to the idea that she might never see her family again. She was a prisoner. The belief that her family would be hurt or killed was firmly planted in her mind. What child would risk bringing harm to the people she loved most?

Brian, Wanda, and Elizabeth walked around Lakeside, California, which is twenty-five miles east of San Diego. Wanda and Elizabeth were forced to wear robes and veils to cover most of their faces whenever they were in public to be certain Elizabeth would never be recognized—even in San Diego. When she wasn't wearing her veil, she usually wore sunglasses. They had set up a campsite that they'd live in for the next four months.

There were occasions when San Diego police directly encountered Mitchell while he held Elizabeth captive. In fact, Brian David Mitchell was arrested on February 12, 2003, for breaking into a church that also housed a preschool. Mitchell was apparently too drunk to carry out his mission of looting the church—he passed out cold. The police found him, woke him, handcuffed him, and brought him to the station for questioning. He gave his name as Michael Jenson. Brian David Mitchell spent six days in jail, where he continued to lie to law-enforcement officials. There was a warrant for his arrest from a misdemeanor shoplifting charge in September, for which Mitchell had failed to appear in court. When police checked his fingerprints, they turned up a name different from the one he'd given—he wasn't Michael Jenson. The police knew the man they had in custody was using an alias. What they never figured out was why.

Elizabeth and Wanda sat alone for those six days, unaware of Brian's whereabouts. Elizabeth was slowly weakening from malnutrition. In an unbelievable bit of irony, Brian David Mitchell was sitting in a jail cell when *America's Most Wanted* aired its second story on him, on February 15, 2003. The show said that Brian David Mitchell was someone the police were seeking to question in connection with Elizabeth's kidnapping. The story pointed out that he sometimes used the name "Immanuel" and that he was traveling with his wife, Wanda Barzee.

For Pete's sake! How much more information did they need? None of the police officers saw the episode of *America's Most Wanted* that night. Since there was no nationwide alert about Mitchell, the Lakeside police were unaware that he was a wanted man. Three days later, Mitchell went before a judge and confessed that he had used terrible judgment by getting drunk the night he broke into the church. He testified that he was a reformed man and wanted to carry out the message given to him by the Lord as to what to do with his life. He pleaded guilty to vandalism, and was given a $250 fine. The judge told Mitchell to go and do the Lord's work but to stop breaking into churches at night. Brian David Mitchell was released from custody.

In this and other instances, Brian David Mitchell had been dismissed as an annoying but harmless street person or as a religious zealot. But he was also a man who could hurt a child. He was a man who could assault a child. The police were wrong.

From the day Elizabeth was taken, leads came pouring in that were fruitless. It was so hard to get our hopes up—even with a sketch of Brian David Mitchell. It wasn't until Mitchell's sister finally called the police and identified the man in the original sketch as her brother that we could put a real name to the face known to us as "Immanuel." She had heard about the sketch and knew it was her brother we were searching for. Even with that information, the police still turned up very little evidence pointing toward him as the perpetrator of the crime. Barzee's sons identified Mitchell after seeing him on *America's Most Wanted* several months later.

The police continued to give us reasons why they could not pursue this very important lead more than they already had. There had been no recent sighting of Brian David Mitchell. He had no known mode of transportation, which meant they were traveling on foot. Logic, statistics, and a lack of evidence precluded the police from looking very intensely. We had heard from a friend of Tom's that a fellow worker at the *Deseret News* had recently hiked up the Bonneville Shoreline Trail, a frequently traveled hiking path behind our house, and had seen Mitchell numerous times over the years. He knew that in previous years Mitchell had kept a tepee up there. When we called the police to inform them that Brian David Mitchell was practically camped in our backyard, they still did nothing.

The day Mitchell was incarcerated, Ed held a news conference to announce that we were ready to reveal the story of "Immanuel." We released the sketch we had and the information that Mary Katherine had identified this man as the man who had taken Elizabeth. We offered a $10,000 reward to anyone who could still vindicate Richard Ricci. Detective Baird was even quoted describing Mitchell as "one of the fifty homeless people who worked on the Smarts' home." Every time we saw Baird appear, we knew disappointment was imminent. Someone had identified Brian David Mitchell from seeing the sketch from the news conference. It was Brian's sister. That was the first time we had a real name for the face. A week later, he was identified again after Wanda Barzee's sons saw *America's Most Wanted*. They called in the tip and positively identified Brian David Mitchell as the man America was looking for. Word was out about Brian David Mitchell.

Doubters were now beginning to come around to the thought that perhaps Richard Ricci was not the man who had taken Elizabeth.

Salt Lake City mayor Rocky Anderson, who was a friend throughout the entire investigation, seemed troubled by the news about Mitchell. He always made time to meet with us. He did what he could do to help the investigation. He kept in touch with Rick Dinse, and one memo he sent to Dinse outlined his concern about the new information pointing toward the man the media knew as "Immanuel." In his memo, the mayor made the following comments:

1. The only eyewitness, Mary Katherine Smart, has maintained from the beginning that she did not think Richard Ricci was the abductor.
2. There is no physical evidence tying Richard Ricci to the abduction.
3. Richard Ricci has no history of sexual abuse or abduction.
4. Mary Katherine independently suggested that the abductor may have been "Immanuel."
5. Immanuel was somewhat familiar with the Smart home.
6. Immanuel has a history of child sexual abuse.
7. Immanuel was seen nearby, at a Kinko's on 1st South Street, near the University of Utah, on the afternoon Elizabeth was abducted.
8. Immanuel was known to camp out near the Bonneville Shoreline Trail, above the Smart home.
9. Perhaps most telling, Immanuel apparently has left the area since information about his possible involvement was disclosed.

FINALLY! Someone from the world of law enforcement would seriously have to take the mayor's points into consideration. The mayor had become outraged by what we had known all along. The Police Department was not aggressively pursuing any angle outside of Richard Ricci, and they were diminishing the relevance of Brian David Mitchell to the case.

As we started to hear unsavory things about Mitchell, we didn't want to believe that Elizabeth was with him. We heard that he had a history of abuse. The police wrote that off to a nasty divorce and an unhappy ex-wife. A few days after hearing the police opinion on stories that were surfacing about Mitchell, we called one of the detectives working on the case and asked if he knew, without a doubt, that Mitchell hadn't been involved in abuse. We needed to know that there was no chance of this allegation being true. The detective professed that he had heard evidence to that effect and that it was his belief that Mitchell had not abused anyone.

"How do you know?"

We were told that one of the officers talked to the ex-wife, and after checking the story, his conclusion was that it was just a nasty divorce.

That wasn't good enough for us.

It was beyond hearsay.

This was our daughter we were fighting for. We'd heard that there had been medical records qualifying the reports of abuse. Had the police checked those out? They had not. As parents we needed hard evidence. We needed to check this out. The thought that our daughter might be in the hands of a known sexual offender was a living nightmare. We pleaded with the officer to follow this through. We needed to know if Elizabeth was with a man who was capable of hurting her—or worse.

Knowing we didn't have the stamina to go through the ups and downs again, Tom and David had taken it upon themselves to talk with Mitchell's family, who had provided photographs of Mitchell for us to look at. Tom e-mailed them to us. When we pulled them up on the computer, we stared in disbelief. It was incredible. To this point, no lead had turned up anything that had potential. We had found the man we were looking for. It was him. We felt sick.

After Elizabeth came home, people would recall that they had seen Brian David Mitchell and two veiled women all around town. The sightings that were later reported in November and December were false, because Brian, Wanda, and Elizabeth were in California. There was a confirmed report that someone had called in a tip about Brian David Mitchell to the Elizabeth Smart kidnapping tip line in August. A lead had come in, but the police were prioritizing the hundreds of leads they had received, and he was not high on the list. In a bizarre twist, it was reported that Brian David Mitchell had walked into the *Deseret News* offices, pulled Elizabeth's Missing poster off the wall, said, "Oh, she's been found," and walked out of the office.

America's Most Wanted aired its third segment about Mitchell on March 1, 2003. This time the show aired photos provided by Wanda Barzee's sons. A nationwide alert about Mitchell and Barzee had been put out. Calls quickly came in from all over; people were recognizing the man we were looking for—and confirming our suspicion and our hope that Elizabeth was in fact alive.

Chapter 20

PRIOR TO KIDNAPPING ELIZABETH, Brian David Mitchell had spent most of his time wandering the streets of Salt Lake City with Wanda Barzee, spouting his own fanatical ramblings. He was directed by prophecy he imagined had been given to him by God. He wrote a lengthy manifesto outlining the details of his mission, extolling the "blessings of polygamy" and calling himself a "just and mighty deity." Somewhere along the line, Mitchell had become convinced that he was the Davidic King. Lacking volunteers willing to join his mission, Mitchell resorted to kidnapping. Though he had set his sights on other young girls, his first real victim was our daughter. Her captivity lasted nine months before they were captured by police in Sandy, Utah, while walking along a highway. They had just arrived back in Salt Lake, having stopped in Las Vegas en route from San Diego.

Several eyewitnesses spotted the three walking the streets. Mitchell and Barzee had Elizabeth in tow, dressed in baggy jeans, a wig, and sunglasses. Witnesses began to call 911 after recognizing Brian David Mitchell from the most recent airing of *America's Most Wanted.* The first call came from Anita and Alvin Dickerson, who had spotted a bearded man and two women walking on the street near a Kinko's in Sandy, Utah. Anita dialed 911 and told the operator she was calling about the man wanted in the Elizabeth Smart kidnapping case. The second call came moments later, from Nancy Montoya, who said she was sitting in her car with her husband and was watching a man who matched the description of the "Immanuel" police were looking for. The Montoyas had first noticed Brian, Wanda, and Elizabeth walking after coming out of the same Kinko's. Nancy seemed to recognize Brian David Mitchell instantly. As they took a better look, her husband agreed—that was him. They immediately called 911.

Sandy police officer Karen Jones was nearby when the 911 calls came in. The sightings were reported over police radios, warning officers in the field to be on the lookout. She was the first police officer to spot Mitchell, Barzee, and Elizabeth the morning of March 12. She, too, thought she recognized him as "Immanuel." She approached the trio and separated Brian David Mitchell for questioning. She asked his name and for some identification. Mitchell responded with a pseudonym, "Peter Marshall." He said his wife's name was Juliette and their daughter was Augustine. His response when asked for identification was: "We are messengers of God. We are free of all worldly things." Elizabeth stood a few feet away, wearing a wig and sunglasses. A second officer approached the scene and made contact with the "daughter" for the first time, thinking she looked a lot like Elizabeth. Officer Jones asked the girl whom she was traveling with. "My parents," Elizabeth said.

Backup was called—Officer Jones alerted the Salt Lake police to the situation. Two more officers arrived on the scene, Victor Quezada and Bill O'Neal. They took turns talking to Brian David Mitchell, Wanda Barzee, and Elizabeth. Officers repeatedly asked the young girl in the veil her name. "Augustine," she said three times. "I know you think I'm that Elizabeth Smart girl who ran away, but I'm not." Officer Troy Rasmussen said he could see her heart beating through her shirt. The police questioned her for forty-five minutes on basic background information about her "parents" and where she was from. They asked her age. "Eighteen," Elizabeth said. Brian had done quite a job on Elizabeth's psyche. She stumbled with her answers, which convinced the officers that something was definitely wrong.

The officers were confused about why Elizabeth was resisting stepping forward and simply identifying who she was and why she wasn't asking for help. Clearly, she was frightened. She was confused, tired, and emotionally battered. They had been traveling—walking and hitchhiking through the desert. She had been physically tied and most certainly was suffering from emotional bondage. She had been gone so many months without anyone finding her that she believed that her plight was never going to end. Police had seen her in the past. Strangers had looked her in the eyes. Even with posters and billboards all around, no one had recognized her as Elizabeth and no one had rescued her. Why would this day be different? If she professed to be Elizabeth Smart that morning and Brian and Wanda were not arrested, Elizabeth was convinced that her life and the lives of her family members were at risk. By that point, Brian David Mitchell had surely convinced Elizabeth that she had no alternative but to stay. Kidnappers threaten their victims emotionally and physically. For nine torturous months, Elizabeth suffered. They can also make their victims feel guilty or ashamed. Those feelings can prevent an abducted child from trying to flee.

The hold that Brian David Mitchell had over Elizabeth was excruciatingly strong. Even when an officer showed her a Missing flier with Elizabeth's image, she denied it was her. When asked about her identity one last time, she finally admitted who she was by proclaiming, "If thou sayeth, I sayeth," and then began to cry. It was over. She was safe. But even then, Elizabeth was unsure if this was really happening. The police tried to explain to her that she was very much loved and missed by everyone—especially her family. It was the beginning of the end of the hellish nightmare we had all been living for nine months. We certainly had no thought about how deeply traumatized Elizabeth would be—we simply wanted her home.

Chapter 21

Ed

March 12, 2003

I was sitting in my office, working, when the phone rang. Lois answered. It was Detective Parks. He told me to drop everything I was doing, don't call anyone, and to go straight to the Sandy police station. I had received so many phone calls like this in the past, I thought nothing of it. I thought I was on my way to identify Brian David Mitchell. It never occurred to me that I was on my way to be reunited with our daughter.

I drove as quickly as I could. I was getting sick inside about not being able to identify the man we had all been looking for. I spoke to Chris Thomas on the way, telling him to cancel two media appearances that we had planned for three o'clock. I told him where I was headed and hung up. Chris called me back to tell me he had heard from a friend at the station that they had a runaway girl in custody who looked a lot like Elizabeth. I didn't get my hopes up too high for fear that once again the lead would turn up nothing. Again, Lois and I had heard this so many times that it still didn't register that it was really Elizabeth. In the days prior, so many sightings of Elizabeth had come in, but most had come from states outside of Utah. I was so desensitized at this point. I couldn't get myself all worked up. I got to the station, still thinking I was there to identify Mitchell.

I wasn't familiar with the Sandy police station. It is in a newer complex that houses city hall, the police station, and other city offices. I kept asking people where to go, and then I finally found an officer who instantly recognized me. "Right this way, Mr. Smart." He eagerly escorted me through the station, past a set of double doors, and past rows of police officers lined up against both sides of the hallway. I didn't think that was normal. Everyone was standing at attention. As we approached a closed-off room, the officer said to me, "We think we found a homeless girl that might be Elizabeth." The door was opened, and I was stunned. I was frozen in disbelief. There, sitting on a sofa, was a girl with her arms folded. She was sitting with a police officer at her side, very quiet and subdued. I stood in the doorway, thinking to myself, "Is this really her?" Was it possible? She had grown so much. She was all grown up. The face resembled our daughter's. The girl sitting in front of me looked so much older; she looked like a homeless girl. She was taller, bigger, more mature-looking. She was unkempt. Her face was round, swollen from being outdoors in the sun. I wasn't certain at first that it was her. I went over and put my arms around her and just started bawling uncontrollably. Was this a dream? Had our nightmare ended? What if this wasn't her?

I held her back, looked her in the eyes, and said, "Is it really you, Elizabeth?"

"Yes, Dad."

I grabbed Elizabeth and held her close to me. I never wanted to let go. I hugged her and told her that I loved her so much.

Our prayers had been answered. Not to have Lois with me was unpardonable. How could the police have not told me to bring my wife? Lois would have crawled on her hands and knees to have been there at that moment. I cried—but for the first time in nine months, my tears were tears of joy.

The detective told me they wanted to transfer Elizabeth. They hurried us to an unmarked car that would take us to the Salt Lake Police Department. I held her tightly as she sat on my lap on the way to Salt Lake City. I called Lois with the miraculous news. I told her we were on our way and that we'd be there in twenty minutes.

Chapter 22

LOIS

*E*D KISSED ME GOOD-BYE and told me he was leaving for the Sandy police station to, he hoped, identify Brian David Mitchell. It was early afternoon, which is the time I usually pick up our younger children from school. After Ed left, his business phone began ringing and at first I didn't think much of it. I rarely answer Ed's business phone, since it rings only in his home office. His phone rings often, but on the afternoon of March 12, it was ringing incessantly—so much so that I finally picked it up and heard:

"This is Lieutenant Jenson. Is this Lois?"

I confirmed it was I.

"Have you heard?"

Heard what?

I could hear him cover the mouthpiece of his phone to say something to another officer—I thought I heard him say, "She doesn't know."

There was a long pause, and then he said, "We think we've found Elizabeth—alive."

I started to shake, and I kept asking the lieutenant if she was okay. I wanted to see her. Charles was working in the yard when he heard me screaming. I didn't want to shout to him what was happening, for fear the neighbors might hear. I asked him to get up to the house as fast as he could. I needed him to drive me to the police station. I was so frantic. I was in no condition to drive. It was a blessing that Charles came home from school early that day. He tried to calm me down, reminding me that we had been through this kind of drill many times—he didn't want me to get my hopes up too high. We had received many phone calls in the previous nine months about young girls the police had found—girls between the ages of fourteen and eighteen. Charles kept reassuring me that everything would be fine. He had certainly grown up over the past nine months. We got into my car, and I don't believe we stopped at a single stop sign. I didn't want to get into an accident and at first kept telling him to slow down, but then I told him to hurry up! While we were driving, Ed called on my cell phone to tell me that he had Elizabeth. It was really her. He said, "You won't believe this, but Elizabeth is here in my arms. I am in Detective Parks's car and we are headed to the Salt Lake station."

I kept asking Ed, "Is it really her? Let me talk to her! I want to talk to Elizabeth."

Some cell phone service in Salt Lake is sketchy at best, so of course when Elizabeth got on the line all I heard was a crackle.

"Elizabeth! Elizabeth! I love you! I love you! Is it really you?" I said, not sure if she could hear me or not. It didn't matter. Our daughter was alive and safe in Ed's arms.

I kept thinking that the sooner we got to the Salt Lake Police Department, the sooner I would see her. I was five minutes away when Ed called, and they were twenty-five minutes from the station. When we arrived at the station, no one said a word. They made us wait. They tried to send us to a room on the sixth floor, but I refused to go. I wanted to be right there in front when Elizabeth walked through that door. Everyone kept trying to pacify me, asking if I would like something to drink, did I need something to eat. NO! I just wanted to see my daughter. They thought it would be better to wait in the privacy of the room on the sixth floor, so I finally agreed and went upstairs. I stood at the window and stared for any sign of my daughter, waiting for what felt like forever. Those twenty minutes seemed equal to the past nine months.

I sent Charles home to get his brothers and sister from school, because they would be waiting for me. They needed to be with us when we were reunited as a family. I knew they'd want to see Elizabeth as much as I did. After Charles left, the mayor of Salt Lake City, Rocky Anderson, arrived at the station. The police station was quickly filling up with officers and investigators. The mayor kept telling me that he wanted to have a welcome-home celebration for Elizabeth. I couldn't focus on anything anyone was saying. All I could think about was Elizabeth.

When they brought Elizabeth to the sixth floor, I was stunned when I saw her for the first time. It was not Elizabeth—at least not my Elizabeth. She was wearing a gray, long sweatshirt that buttoned up the front, and an old worn pair of jeans that were being held up by a rope. Her hair was in two French braids—a way she had never worn her hair before she was taken. Her face was puffy—she was sunburned. She was so much bigger than I remembered. Her shoulders had developed from carrying a heavy backpack—she had grown and developed in the nine months she was gone. *This* Elizabeth didn't look anything like the little girl in the Missing posters. It was very hard to see her like that. I grabbed Elizabeth and hugged her as tightly as I could. She held on to me, digging her fingers into my back. I never wanted to let her go, nor did she want to let me go.

A few minutes after our reunion, the police took Elizabeth away, explaining that they needed to get her statement while her memory was still fresh and untainted. Not knowing that we didn't have to let the officers interview her, we allowed the police to take her away. Chris Thomas handed Ed his cell phone—John Walsh had heard that Elizabeth had been found and he was on the phone. Ed said to John, "You're not going to believe this, but she is here. Elizabeth is here. The police are interviewing her right now." Both Ed and I were worried about the police handling Elizabeth without one of us present. John explained that the police absolutely did not have to question Elizabeth right at that moment. He told Ed to go get her and protect her from the questioning, which would surely be intrusive if not damaging.

Ed flew into an absolute rage—behavior that is not typical for my husband. He was yelling at everyone. "Put a stop to this right now!" he shouted. Ed saw Police Chief Rick Dinse, FBI Investigator Chip Beirus, and Mayor Rocky Anderson and began demanding that they get our daughter. He was pounding his fists on the table and demanding to stop the interview with Elizabeth. I certainly didn't want the media to see Ed in this condition. Ed later told me that his rage was heightened because he couldn't shake his thoughts about how appalling the line of questioning had been for our family when Elizabeth was taken. He couldn't bear the thought of Elizabeth being put through that kind of interrogation. She was the victim. Ed had never shared his phone call with John Walsh with me, so I had no idea why he was losing his composure. This was a time that we should have been rejoicing in privacy as a family. Instead, we were once again being subjected to someone else's agenda. The thought of what Elizabeth had gone through and the potential leaks had pushed Ed over the edge.

They finally brought Elizabeth back to us, and that's when her brothers and sister saw her for the first time. They hugged her and held her and told her how much they loved her. We were so happy to have her home. To rejoice, we knelt down in the middle of the police station and had a family prayer. All of our children were there—we knelt in a circle and thanked God for this miracle. This was truly an incredible moment.

The police station was now packed with people. The word had spread that Elizabeth had been found. A huge crowd had gathered outside the station. The entire block was packed with people. Once again, news vans and satellite trucks had converged on Salt Lake City. This time it was to celebrate that Elizabeth was home. Sadly, our own celebration would have to wait. The police insisted on getting more testimony from Elizabeth before they would release her for a medical examination. They would not allow Ed and me to both be present during her questioning. The police stood firm that if they were to bring charges against Brian David Mitchell and Wanda Barzee, Elizabeth's statements were crucial. They didn't want her recollection to be corrupted by media or other outside influences. That explanation seemed to make some sense to us, so I agreed to accompany her for questioning. To my utter disbelief, they would not let me sit with Elizabeth during the questioning. I was allowed to witness everything from a room that had a small television monitor, which I could barely hear. I was told that the volume control was broken, but I am not convinced that was the case. Listening to Elizabeth tell of the nightmare she had suffered through for nine months was the hardest thing I have ever done in my life. I felt like dying as I listened to my daughter painstakingly detail the abuse and assault she endured at the hands of Brian David Mitchell and Wanda Barzee. I will never forget the sinking feeling I had watching my daughter tell of her living hell. As she spoke, I remember feeling that Wanda Barzee was just as despicable as Brian Mitchell; as a woman—as a mother—how could she have allowed this to happen to a young girl? To someone's daughter?

The police finally allowed us to leave the station around seven o'clock. Though they tried to shield us from the hordes of press and media that had now gathered outside the station, some clever photographer still found a way to shoot us as we made our way to the back of a windowless van that was to take us to the hospital for a medical examination. Elizabeth and I sat in the back of the van, looking out the front windshield, passing billboards and posters that bore Elizabeth's image. I explained that the whole country had been praying for her. I told her the light blue ribbons that were hanging all over town were in her honor. Elizabeth said she had noticed them over the nine months but never realized they were for her.

"I thought light blue was appropriate, since it's your favorite color."

"Mom, light blue is not my favorite color! Why would you pick light blue?"

We passed by her junior high school, and there was a banner strewn across the fence that said, "We Love You Liz!"

And suddenly, it sunk in. Elizabeth was home—really home.

We were taken to the University Hospital in Salt Lake, where we were whisked through a private door and down a corridor that was virtually empty. Elizabeth was given a complete physical. Thank heavens she was healthy. Her diet had been limited while she had been held captive. Elizabeth ate one meal a day, and that was usually bread. She wasn't able to get much exercise, since she usually sat around tethered by a cable. When she did come down from the canyon, she walked and was forced to carry a heavy backpack. I could see Elizabeth was uncomfortable, so I tried to get her through the medical exam as quickly as possible. The hospital staff was able to come up with a pair of sweatpants and a clean T-shirt so Elizabeth could get out of the smelly, grungy, dirty clothes she had been in for too many months. It must have felt good to put on clean clothes.

Finally, at approximately ten o'clock in the evening, Elizabeth and I were able to head home. She wanted to go home. We started toward our neighborhood in the same van that took us to the hospital, and someone stopped us to say that we couldn't get up the street because there were too many reporters blocking the road. That was simply ridiculous. It was out of the question that Elizabeth couldn't be taken straight home. I demanded that the police make way for us—they had the authority to move all of those people. I called Ed, who had taken the other children home when Elizabeth and I went to the hospital, and told him to open the garage door so the van could pull right in. Elizabeth was entitled to have some privacy in her homecoming. We had so little privacy left; it was the least they could do to grant us this moment of bringing our daughter home in peace.

We walked through the door to see the faces of her brothers and sister. Our extended family and friends had made banners and hung balloons all up and down our street. There were blue ribbons tied on the handrails of the steps leading to our home. Fresh ribbons could be seen up and down our street, tied to trees, bushes, and lampposts.

The first thing Elizabeth wanted to do was take a bath. I drew the biggest bubble bath I had ever made in my large Jacuzzi tub. The dirt, grime, and soot that sat at the bottom of the tub when she finished her bath was thick and muddy. She washed her hair over and over again, giving new meaning to the phrase "rinse and repeat." I don't think she felt totally clean for a solid week! She basically hadn't bathed in nine months. Elizabeth had been living out in the wild. If she was lucky, once a week Brian and Wanda gave her a cold bucket of water to pour over her head.

After Elizabeth bathed, she wanted to play a piece on her harp. She struggled through a song and realized she was a bit out of practice. She looked up at all of us and said, "Well, it's been nine months!" It was wonderful to see that she hadn't lost her sense of humor.

Around midnight, we all piled on my bed and Elizabeth asked if we could watch the tape of one of her favorite movies, *The Trouble with Angels*. The children gathered round—some on the bed and others on the floor—and for the first time in nine months we were back to being a regular family. I was certain that Elizabeth would be sleeping in our room that first night home. I couldn't imagine her wanting to go back to the bed from which she had been taken. However, when the movie ended, Elizabeth got up as if nothing had ever happened, and said she was tired and ready for bed. We all knelt down to give thanks to our Heavenly Father for this miracle.

"Mom, don't worry. I'm just fine. I'm going to be safe. I'm going to be here in the morning."

I will never forget those words.

She kissed us good night and went to her room. We didn't quite know what to say except "Good night and we love you." As you might expect, we spent most of the night checking in on her—just to be sure.

For me, the nine months Elizabeth was gone in a way mirrored my pregnancy with her. Even though I didn't get to see her, I knew that she was there. When your child goes missing, in a way the umbilical cord is reattached and is far more difficult to cut. After Elizabeth came home, the cord was stronger than ever.

The next morning, when Mary Katherine awoke, she said she had had the best night of sleep ever. For the first time in nine months, she didn't need her night-light. She said her prayers had been answered, because Elizabeth had come home.

And I will also ease the burdens which are put upon your shoulders, that
even you cannot feel them upon your backs, even while you are in bondage;
and this will I do that ye may stand as witnesses for me hereafter, and that
ye may know of a surety that I, the Lord God, do visit my people in their
afflictions.

—Mosiah 24:14

The Lord had strengthened my heart while Elizabeth was gone so that I could bear my burdens. The beginning of her healing had already started with the many prayers that were being said on her behalf.

The odds were heavily stacked against bringing Elizabeth home. Even if we were fortunate enough to find her, what kind of damage would she have suffered? Most kids who are recovered suffer indelible long-term effects from their trauma. I don't know that any of us understand the full magnitude of what we all experienced during those nine months and the several months since Elizabeth has come home. I have my daughter back—the most glorious resolution I could have ever hoped for. With God's help, we will survive.

Chapter 23

One soul is lost, an angel is missing.
Which mother's grieving is more?
Hearts unite in Love and Prayer
Thousands, Millions petition the Lord
How often one's faith is extended and strengthened
On the road of our early estate
We pray for the lost soul to return to the fold.
Life's journey has not yet ended.

—ED SMART, 2002

*B*RINGING ELIZABETH HOME would seem like a logical place to end our journey. In truth, we would have loved nothing more than to have our daughter back and move on with our lives. But that isn't the reality of the situation we faced after Elizabeth came home. We know what it's like to lose a child—to have a stranger snatch her right out from under our watchful eyes. There can be no real end to our story until there is an end to the plight of missing children. We are one of the few fortunate families who got their missing child back. How can we expect to have no involvement in crusading for the well-being of all missing children?

The Rachael Alert had just been put into place in Utah in April 2002, three months before Elizabeth was taken. It was named for Rachael Runyan, a four-year-old girl who had been kidnapped and found dead. The Rachael Alert had gone out four hours after we reported Elizabeth missing. It was the first time Utah had put the system to use. There are certain criteria that must be met before the police will activate the alert. First, they need to determine that the child is a minor or is mentally handicapped. Second, they need to establish that the missing child is in imminent danger. Third, they must be certain it is not a runaway situation—that the child has in fact been abducted. And, fourth, a description of the missing child has to be complete. Without establishing these guidelines, the alert would be useless—there would be too many alerts for the system to be effective. What it boils down to is having educated law enforcement that can quickly determine whether the situation meets the criteria. Elizabeth's photo had been released to the media hours before the statewide alert went out. Why it took so long when the eyewitness said Elizabeth had been taken at gunpoint seemed a mystery. The fact is that human judgment is a critical element in deciding whether the criteria are met for sending out an alert. Granted, we hope this doesn't become such a common occurrence, but training and the ability to recognize the criteria make the difference between minutes and hours, the difference between life and death. The police were uncertain she was in danger and had been abducted, so there was hesitation in sending out the alert. Since Elizabeth's abduction, Utah has made tremendous improvements by upgrading their system (which later became the Amber Alert) with the finest state-of-the-art technology.

California, which was in the process of getting its alert system off the ground when Utah sent out the alert about Elizabeth, wanted to glean everything it could from what Utah had done in order to make its system successful. Following Elizabeth's abduction, the state implemented a public-alert system using electronic highway signs and private electronic signs volunteered by their owners. The alert system is not a cure-all—it doesn't catch everyone, but it remains in a state of evolution, with many people's continual efforts making it more effective. And most important, *it does something.* That is a comfort to the families whose children go missing. When it works, it brings children home.

We never want to see any parent go through what we have been through as parents of a missing child. For Ed, getting involved with the Amber Alert has become an ongoing effort. It is an issue that has been debated for years and has finally received the attention it deserves. We often wondered how quickly a unified alert system would pass through Congress if a child of a representative or senator had been kidnapped. This was something that could have been taken care of a long time ago. We must have a potential safety net out there. We lobbied Washington to make several attempts to meet with the right people to try and push the Amber Alert. We felt strongly that there was something good we could do as a result of Elizabeth's disappearance. We met with staff members, who were always cordial and both politically and diplomatically correct, but were not the people who could make changes in Washington.

When Elizabeth came home, Ed directed his frustration directly at Congressman Jim Sensenbrenner. It seemed the head of the Judiciary Committee had the ultimate power. It was clear that something had to be done in Washington to get the standalone Amber Alert bill pushed through. The process was taking so long. Sensenbrenner's position could allow the bill to go through. He was holding the trump card to make it happen. He refused to play. He wouldn't meet with us. His aide said that he didn't want to make this a political issue. He was receiving negative coverage in his local media. He warned us that this issue would promptly be placed at the bottom of his to-do list if that happened again. How does anything ever pass through the system? Something as important as saving children put at the bottom of the pile? We couldn't force anyone, but we knew we could get their attention.

At the time, the Senate again voted unanimously for the bill. Congress had voted for the Child Protection Act, which encompasses so much more than the Amber Alert—but the two entities were at loggerheads. We had pushed with Martin Frost and Congresswoman Dunn for a petition for isolating the Amber Alert from the Child Protection Act, which would have moved the bill through the system faster. It was time for the leaders of this country to act like leaders.

This should have been a nonpartisan issue—there was no question that everyone wanted it—but it got clogged in the wheels of legislation. We implored Congressman Chris Cannon, Senator Hatch, Senator Bennett, and Jim Matheson to help. We still had a fair amount of press covering Elizabeth's disappearance, so we were able to get the media to cover our efforts. The media definitely helped us to pass that bill into law. It filled our hearts to continually hear success stories, knowing that children could be saved. These children who were missing were not just being held hostage by their abductors—they were hostages of the system.

When Elizabeth came home, Ed was so elated to have her back that, in a statement to the press, he asked that we all think of the parents out there who are not as lucky as we were to have our child home.

There are missing children right now and there are children who will go missing in the future, that will be abducted tomorrow. We, the people of America, have a chance to make a difference. It's called the Amber Alert. The blood of those children will be on your head, Jim Sensenbrenner. You are halting this. Leaders need to step up to the plate. They need to be leaders. Do what you need to do to make this happen. Call your congressman. This saves lives. Don't let another death happen because of your unwillingness to change.

This statement raised a lot of eyebrows in Washington. Ed continuously made this point the night Elizabeth came home and the next morning during the rounds of talk-show appearances. If that is what it took to get this bill passed, then so be it. We, along with Elizabeth, wrote a letter to Congress, asking them to please bring the Amber Alert as a standalone bill. We wanted to get the job done. We heard our letter was read on the floor.

March 18, 2003
An Open Letter to the House of Representatives:
Thank you very much for your continued support and warm wishes over the past nine months. We especially appreciate all the representatives who are working together to diligently pass the National Amber Alert Legislation.

Today, Elizabeth was introduced to the Amber Alert when she asked about a videotape in my office. After watching the coverage, Elizabeth asked why the legislation has not passed when it saves so many children's lives. I could not give her an answer!

After a lengthy conversation about how the Amber Alert has been politicized, she asked me if there was anything she could do to help it pass. We decided to draft this letter.

As you know, I can't express enough how our children can't wait another day for the National Amber Alert to be signed into law by President Bush. Please, please, please pass the standalone Amber Alert legislation NOW! As soon as you do, I will be there to celebrate and then will go on to work with you on lobbying the Senate to pass other pending issues for our children.

I wish to apologize to anyone who was offended by my excitement last week. You cannot comprehend the joy of having your child return. The Amber Alert will make this a reality for countless families. Please don't underestimate the immediacy and power of this legislation!

This is your opportunity to show your leadership for our children. We look forward to seeing you soon.

Sincerely,

Ed, Lois and Elizabeth Smart

It looked as if our efforts were beginning to pay off. It was becoming clear that Washington was willing to compromise and go into conference on the larger bill. But then I received a distressing call from John Walsh, who seemed certain the issue was dead. The following day, the bill went to the Senate floor and was openly debated between Senator Ted Kennedy and Senator Orrin Hatch. At the end of Senator Hatch's presentation, he called for a vote and the bill was unanimously passed.

We were so grateful for the bill passing, which protects the rights and freedom of all the children in the United States. To hear about the bipartisan effort in which egos were put aside and the right thing was finally done was overwhelming. Our hat goes off to the many people who made this happen, including Congressman Jim Sensenbrenner, who fought for the bigger picture, Congressman Martin Frost, Congresswoman Jennifer Dunn, Senator Orrin Hatch, Senator Joe Biden, Senator Patrick Leahy, and so many others who worked behind the scenes and came together to protect those young people who are our future.

We would like all parents of missing children to have their children safely home. We won't rest until this country has a unified interstate alert system. It seems such an easy thing to set up. What could be more important than the safety of our children? After Elizabeth was rescued, we were invited to Washington, D.C., to witness President George Bush sign the Child Protection Act, including the Amber Alert bill, into law.

The White House was incredible. We never dreamed we'd be there. We met President Bush in a private room and spoke with him for a half hour. Other parents of missing children were there as well. Some parents had children who had been rescued and others still had missing children, and there were two young girls there who had been students at Cal-Poly when they had been kidnapped while sitting in a car with some friends. One of the girls approached Elizabeth and told her how happy she was to meet her and that she was more excited to meet Elizabeth than she was President Bush! The truth is, we were all eager to meet one another at the White House, having been through the summer of missing children. It was very touching.

We were so proud to witness the signing of the Child Protection Act, especially having Elizabeth at our side.

Later that day, Elizabeth was asked to play the harp for a special segment of *The John Walsh Show*. She was radiant, all in white, as she performed with the Capitol building as her backdrop.

After we returned home from Washington, it didn't take long for the D.A.'s investigators to make a point of telling us that the hardest part of our journey lies ahead—the trial. Incredibly, they told us that the kidnapping was a breeze compared to the struggles we'll face if and when Brian David Mitchell and Wanda Barzee go to trial. Obviously, we don't accept that anything could be as bad as having lost Elizabeth. But the subject of victims' rights has become of particular interest to us in the past few months. As we face the upcoming trial, our eyes have been opened to the shortcomings of the judicial process as it pertains to a victim of a crime. Victims of crime have long been on the receiving end of neglect from legislators and mistreatment from members of the criminal justice system. They are most often relegated to enduring the consequences of the crime committed against them without any support or assistance. Victims are often treated without any dignity or respect by law enforcement as well as members of the media—something we became all too familiar with during the investigation as the parents of a victim.

Unfortunately, victims deal with the frustration of immediately becoming inactive participants, forced to take a peripheral role in the legal process. In Elizabeth's case, it would be a blessing that she would not be exposed to a cruel reenactment of the ordeal in the courtroom. The case becomes a legal matter between the defendant and the state, leaving victims excluded from decisions about charges being brought against the defendants. They often have little or no influence over the prosecution for their case, no right to choose legal representation, and no right to appeal because there are no federal laws on the books to ensure anything. We personally have hired legal representation, but for most victims it is not a given. Not only has the victim gone through the pain of a horrifying criminal act, but they are then also forced to suffer future victimization during the justice process. The bottom line is that crime does not victimize only one person. Grief-stricken family members may be considered indirect victims as well: mothers, fathers, wives, husbands, brothers, sisters, and children.

For too long, our criminal justice system has failed to recognize the dignity, welfare, and understanding of the living victims left to deal with overwhelming tragedy. They are left with no right to due process, no right to a lawyer, no right to privacy, no right to be informed and consulted, no right to access the court record, and no right to the finality of their traumatic ordeal. The criminal acts through its destructive path, leaving victims as mere "evidence."

Why shouldn't it be federal law that victims receive timely notice of any release, escape, and public proceeding involving the crime? Why should victims often not be allowed to speak at release, plea, sentencing, commutation, and pardon proceedings?

All of the foregoing constitutional rights are granted to accused offenders:

1. The U.S. Constitution guarantees more than a dozen rights to those accused of committing crimes.
2. Victims' rights are secondary to the constitutional rights of defen-

dants, as well as secondary to the interest of judges and lawyers, some of whom are insensitive and have their own agendas.

3. A new sensitivity to victims' rights can be brought about only by ensuring that the U.S. Constitution guarantees their right to be treated with fairness, dignity, and respect.

At the moment, criminal justice seems like justice for criminals. Approximately 9 percent of reported violent crimes are resolved with the perpetrator being incarcerated. In turn, this influences the justice process, because it affects the victims' decisions of whether or not to come forward when a crime has been committed.

Currently, fourteen states have enacted constitutional amendments for the rights of victims. In addition, Patrick Leahy (D-VT) introduced the "Crime Victims Assistance Act of 2003" on April 7, 2003, which aims to enhance the rights of crime victims and to establish grants for local governments to assist crime victims.

GENERAL VICTIMS' RIGHTS
ONLY SOME STATES ABIDE BY

1. To be treated with fairness, respect, and dignity and to have a swift and fair resolution of your case
2. To be informed of and present at all critical stages of the criminal justice process
3. To be present and heard in court for any bond reduction, amendment of charges, disposition, sentencing, or continuances
4. To have a safe waiting area near the court

5. To confer with the District Attorney's Office before the case is resolved or goes to trial, and to be informed of the outcome

6. To prepare a Victim Impact Statement and to be present at sentencing

7. To have restitution ordered

8. To pursue a civil judgment against anyone who has committed a crime against you

9. To be informed of post-conviction release or modification hearings

10. To get your property back quickly when it is no longer needed for prosecution

11. To apply for Victim Compensation for crime-related losses such as therapy, medical, and funeral expenses

As parents, we strongly urge you to get involved with your legislators on the issue of victims' rights. Write your congressman, your senator, the President of the United States, and tell him or her that you think the time has come to make changes in the system to protect the victim—not the defendant. If it were your child, what would you do?

CRIME VICTIMS' RIGHTS AMENDMENT
PROPOSED IN APRIL 2003

The U.S. Constitution, mainly through *amendments*, grants those accused of crime many rights, such as a speedy trial, a jury trial, counsel, the right against self-incrimination, the right to be free from unreasonable searches and seizures, the right to subpoena witnesses, the right to confront witnesses, and the right to due process under the law. The same document, however, guarantees no rights to crime victims. Victims have no right to be present, no right to be informed of hearings, no right to be heard at sentencing or at a parole hearing, no right to insist on reasonable conditions of release to protect the victim, no right to restitution, no right to challenge unending delays in the disposition of their case, and no right to be told if they might be in danger from release or escape of their attacker. The Crime Victims' Rights Amendment would bring a new balance to the judicial system.

RIGHTS IN THE AMENDMENT

The amendment gives victims of violent crime the right:

1. To reasonable and timely notice of any public proceeding involving the crime and of any release or escape of the accused
2. Reasonably to be heard at public release, plea, sentencing, reprieve, and pardon proceedings
3. To adjudicative decisions that duly consider the victim's safety, interest in avoiding unreasonable delay, and just and timely claims to restitution from the offender

In the 106th Congress, Senators Dianne Feinstein and Jon Kyl introduced S.J. Res. 3, the Crime Victims' Rights Constitutional Amendment, which was cosponsored by a bipartisan group of forty-one senators, including Senators Biden, Reid, Lieberman, Lott,

McCain, Craig, and Snowe. Governors in forty-nine out of fifty states have called for an amendment. In 2000, forty-three attorneys general (including three federal) endorsed the amendment. There is strong support around the country for an amendment. Thirty-two states have passed similar measures—by an average popular vote of almost 80 percent.

In April 2003, Senator Kyl talked at length about fundamental reform of the criminal justice system, which can be brought about only by changes in the fundamental law—the Constitution. He said that attempts to establish rights by federal or state statute, or even state constitutional amendment, have proved inadequate after more than twenty years of trying. Rights that are guaranteed by the Constitution will provide for a national baseline. According to a report by the National Institute of Justice, even in states that had victims' rights legislation, fewer than 60 percent of the victims were notified of the sentencing hearing and fewer than 40 percent were notified of the release of the defendant.

The Crime Victims' Rights Amendment has strong support in the House and Senate and from the International Association of Chiefs of Police and major national victims' rights groups, including Parents of Murdered Children, the National Organization for Victim Assistance, Mothers Against Drunk Driving (MADD), the Maryland Crime Victims' Resource Center, Arizona Voice for Crime Victims, Crime Victims United, and Memory of Victims Everywhere.

Chapter 24

Sing, O Heavens; and be joyful, O earth . . . for the Lord hath comforted his people . . . I will save thy children . . . and all flesh shall know that I the Lord am thy Saviour and thy Redeemer . . .

—Isaiah 49:13, 25–26

A MIRACLE!"

The headlines around the world on March 13, 2003, rang of words like "Miracle," "Answered Prayers," and "She's Home!" Elizabeth had been found alive in nearby Sandy, Utah. Her safe return came just as the country was facing imminent war, threats of terrorism, and economic doom. The word that Elizabeth had been found diverted the attention of Americans to some happy news. It was an absolute miracle. We proclaimed loudly and proudly, "God lives! He answers prayers!"

Though we had been willing to accept any outcome, we firmly believe that faith and prayers had an influence in bringing our daughter home. Throughout the nine months, we could feel our Heavenly Father's love. We are so thankful to Him for the abundance of blessings that were poured down on us and continue to be now that Elizabeth is home.

At the first candlelight vigil for Elizabeth in June 2002, a jazz singer sang "Amazing Grace." At the time, we had no idea how appropriate that choice would be. With Elizabeth's homecoming, the words "I once was lost and now I'm found" took on a whole new meaning. Elizabeth didn't attend the homecoming vigil, but she wanted to send a message to the world. We thought she would need some help writing something, but she didn't. Without hesitation, Elizabeth took a pen and inscribed the message she felt from her heart. She wrote on a large poster board, "I am the luckiest girl in the world! Thank you for your love and prayers. It's a wish come true. I'm home! I love you all. Elizabeth Smart." We had a police escort to Liberty Park. When we got there, thousands of people were there to welcome Elizabeth home. People were hugging and crying and were sharing their joy and jubilation.

Rocky Anderson spoke to the crowd first. Lois took the stage, and in reference to Elizabeth's message raised her arms in the air and said, "And I'm the luckiest mother in the world!" She shared with the crowd that Elizabeth was doing all the girly things—taking long bubble baths, painting her nails, and catching up on all the movies she had missed over the nine months. She was doing all the things a fifteen-year-old girl likes to do. Ed spoke next, thanking everyone and expressing his hope that the congressional leadership in the Senate and House would step up to be the leaders we need them to be. They don't represent themselves. They represent us. He told the crowd that God lives, and for those who had doubt, He does answer prayers. John Walsh, who flew to Salt Lake after hearing the news that Elizabeth had been found, spoke next. Before the celebration ended, Ed asked the crowd to stop for a moment and pray for all the parents of missing children so they, too, could have a miracle in their lives. He also asked for the crowd to pray for President Bush, as we were a country about to go to war and we had to remember those servicemen and -women who were fighting for our freedom.

We went home after the celebration and were shocked at the continuous outpouring of love from everyone. We received more than seventy floral arrangements, including one with Elizabeth's image on the petals. We also received hundreds of stuffed animals and angels, among them a life-sized moose sent by one well-wisher from Park City. We thought about bringing the flowers and stuffed animals to local hospitals because they were crowding us out of our home. But we wanted Elizabeth to know and understand how much she was missed and loved. She will perhaps never fully understand the enormity of her abduction, but a letter she received from someone in Egypt after she returned has given her some insight. This was the first time she felt the love and prayers of so many people who had hoped and prayed for her while she was missing. It felt good to all of us, but Elizabeth was truly touched.

When Elizabeth came home, we received numerous phone calls from family and friends—and even one from the President of the

United States. Mrs. Bush had called to express her worry when Elizabeth was initially taken. We were touched by the Bushes' warmth and sincerity. Lois was bathing when our son Edward called upstairs to tell her that she had a phone call. Lois yelled back down, "Not now! Take a message." Edward explained that he thought it was someone important because they insisted on speaking to one of us. Lois decided to reach for the phone, but as she did, Edward hung up the extension in the kitchen—not realizing he had just hung up on the White House. After that, Ed received a call on his cell phone. The voice on the other end said that the President wanted to talk to him. The President expressed how thrilled he was that Elizabeth was home. He called it a miracle—and it truly was.

All kinds of people lent their support to our family when Elizabeth was missing. B.A.C.A., which stands for Bikers Against Child Abuse, is a group that has always been a strong children's advocate. These guys were there for our family from the day Elizabeth was kidnapped. At the homecoming vigil, one of the bikers handed us a white tapered candle the group had saved from the first candlelight vigil. They wanted us to have the candle to enjoy as a token of their support. And when Brian David Mitchell and Wanda Barzee were charged with their crimes, B.A.C.A. showed up on the courthouse steps to represent all missing and abused children. We love you, B.A.C.A. boys!

On March 18, 2003, Brian David Mitchell and Wanda Barzee were charged with six felony counts. David Yocum, the Salt Lake County district attorney, is seeking life sentences for the two, who are behind bars on $10 million bail. The case is currently a state issue, but federal charges could be brought against the two in the future. In addition to the kidnapping and aggravated sexual assault charges, Mitchell and Barzee face aggravated burglary charges for breaking into our home using a dangerous weapon, another charge of aggravated burglary for attempting to break into our relatives' home while Elizabeth was being held against her will, and a second charge of aggravated kidnapping for attempting to abduct Elizabeth's cousin. The severity of the charges is an indication of the danger that Mitchell and Barzee presented throughout the nine months Elizabeth was gone.

Since Mitchell and Barzee have been taken into custody, relatives of Mitchell's have come forward and have described him as a religious extremist. Mitchell has explained in a "manifesto" he wrote that he was acting on his own. Mitchell was not just a zealot looking for converts, he was a sexual predator. He was aided and was abetted in his actions by Wanda Barzee. To us, they are both equally culpable.

"I feel triumphant!"

Those were the words Elizabeth spoke the day she took us to see the campsite where she had been held captive. It was amazing to be there with her and to witness her feeling that she had conquered Mitchell and Barzee. Ed and Elizabeth have gone jogging together several times after she returned home. Sometimes they run up one of the canyons behind our home—in the hills where Elizabeth was held. We thought that maybe, someday, she'd want to take us there, but we never expected to have Elizabeth, just a couple of weeks after coming home, want to show us where she was held captive. When Elizabeth came home it was like having a newborn baby, so to speak, since we worried about her all the time. We thought the visit to the campsite would set her back—that she wouldn't be able to deal with it. We gave her plenty of opportunity to bow out—but it was important to Elizabeth that we see the site. She was adamant. She wanted to go. "I want to do it now," she said.

Everyone in the family except William and Edward hiked up the trail together. Elizabeth marched up that hill as if she were headed to battle. We arrived, and she showed us everything: "This is the place we hid our shoes. This is where we got water. This is where I lived." We were stunned at the calm and secure way that Elizabeth spoke. She explained that she, Brian, and Wanda had moved between two campsites. The upper site is where she was for the first two months. Then, Brian moved them to a lower campsite. He obviously felt safe with what he was doing by the time they moved to the lower camp. It had been two months and nobody had found them. It is so unbelievable that thousands of searchers were looking for Elizabeth—any sign of her—and no one found her. Elizabeth has said that Brian constantly reinforced that it was God's will that no one would catch him, that God had told him to take Elizabeth. When we stood at the site, Elizabeth was free—free to do and say whatever she wanted. It was liberating and cathartic. More crucial to her was to prove that Brian and Wanda did not own her. There were no tears—she certainly didn't show any anguish about being there. It was like a cleansing for her. It is part of the healing. For us, it was bewildering. We didn't know what to expect. It was horrifying seeing the conditions she had to live under. On the other hand, it was glorious to see our daughter hold her head up in victory—to see her in control, knowing that she was a survivor in every sense of the word.

It was a continuation of the rebirth of Elizabeth Ann Smart.

Today, Elizabeth is trying to get back to normal. She is so looking forward to getting her driver's license. She is now sixteen years old. It has been a year and a half since she was kidnapped. Life has changed for all of us. But Elizabeth is reconnecting with her friends—trying to catch up on the year she missed out on in their lives. She's not allowed to date until she's sixteen, which means by the time you read this book, our daughter will most likely be driving and dating—yikes! She's right on target—doing the things she ought to be doing. She goes out with her friends, which is sometimes hard for us, but we want life to be sweet for her. She started school in the fall, and is adjusting well to being back in the swing of things.

Chapter 25

ELIZABETH

*D*EAR WORLD:

I am so happy and thankful to be home with the people I love.
I'm doing great. I owe a lot to my family and to the great friends
that I have. I want to thank them for not giving up on me. I wish I
could thank each and every person who prayed for me individually.
If you were standing in front of me now, I'd shake your hand and tell
you how much your good thoughts and prayers meant to my family
and me.

Through my experience, I have learned not to take anything for granted—not my life, my family, my safety, my health, my friends, or even my enemies. You have to live life every day knowing how precious God's gifts are. I also believe that you have to live your life without fear and anger. If you fear something enough, I think you can sometimes make that fear a reality. If today were your last day on earth, would you have told the people you love that you love them? Would you have any regrets? Would you be able to die peacefully and without a grudge? I have learned that living in the moment means taking the time to do the things that are meaningful and important. Every day is a blessing. I feel so blessed to be back home, with my family and friends. I truly am the luckiest girl in the world! Thank you for all of your love and support.

Chapter 26

LOTS OF CHILDREN have been kidnapped. Is that predestination? We don't think we were predestined to go through this. We believe that God knows all. He knows from beginning to end our thoughts, our prayers, our hopes, dreams, plans, everything. He knows and understands each of us so well. He knows how we will react and endure in any situation. We relied upon our faith to sustain us. We truly believe in a God in Heaven who loves us all—who is there for us. We never walk alone. That is how we made it. That is how we survived. God knows the larger picture. Maybe our experience was meant to touch many people. Maybe that's the reason Elizabeth was taken. We will never know.

We received a very moving and memorable letter from a young man who had proclaimed himself an atheist his entire life. He was riveted by our story and the disappearance of Elizabeth. He was drawn to this situation when he had never cared about a kidnapped or missing child in the past. He was consumed with the story. He wrote that every night he checked the news to see if there had been a break in the case. He found himself on his knees praying for Elizabeth to be found. He was praying to God. He had been an atheist his whole life, but through Elizabeth's story, he realized he did believe in God. He believed that miracles can happen. He is now convinced that there is a higher power that is involved in our lives.

We are all here for a purpose—it's not just chance that we come here. Maybe Elizabeth's kidnapping was God's way of showing the world that He can perform miracles. It refined us. It brought us together as a nation of faithful people from all religions and beliefs. It gave us hope. It made us better people. It made our family more believing and trusting in God. We had a miraculous firsthand experience. There is no way we could have brought Elizabeth home on our own.

There were many miracles throughout the nine months that Elizabeth was gone. But even if we hadn't brought Elizabeth home, the miracles would have still been there. If we look at life only in terms of our mortal existence, then of course those who don't have their children return do not experience a miracle. But they do, because they are given the strength to carry on even in the absence of their child. We know this because we accepted the notion that Elizabeth might never come back. We became stronger in our faith through that experience. If a miracle is viewed in terms of immortality and eternal life, which is what our family believes, the miracle exists in every respect. In death, severe illness, even kidnapping, miracles do happen.

Looking back on the experience, we know that none of us will ever be the same. We are stronger for what we've experienced. Our love is stronger and our faith is deeper. We have great hope for the future. We will continue to seek the Lord and stay the course. We have all been in situations where we've felt lost from time to time. We pray to be rescued from those days of waiting and watching, feeling misplaced, hoping to be stronger. We all stumble along in fear and confusion, hoping our steps will lead us to a better place. We all sometimes need a miracle rescue—let Elizabeth's story be a reminder of the possibility of miracles. Elizabeth has been in therapy since the end of her ordeal. It's fair to say that when she talks about her kidnapping, it is difficult, especially when she details the events of those nine months to investigators and lawyers.

We will continue to get Elizabeth all the help she needs to be certain she will be equipped to handle the road ahead in life. It will be a long road until the time Elizabeth is fully recovered, but we will be by her side—together as a family to help support her, love her, and see to it that she has a wonderful life.

Acknowledgments

W<small>E WANT TO GIVE</small> our deepest gratitude to our Heavenly Father, for His love and guidance, and for the spirit and belief that we would emerge from this experience stronger, wiser, and full of love and hope that prayers are answered and miracles do happen.

There are so many people we'd like to thank for all of their love, prayers, support, donations, and help while Elizabeth was missing. Our family was deeply touched by everyone's generosity and selflessness during that time. We could never have imagined that so many people from all faiths, religious backgrounds, and different walks of life would have come together with the common goal of helping bring our daughter home. It would be nearly impossible to thank each of you individually, though we truly wish we could. Thank you to all of our family members—especially our parents, Charles and Dorotha, and Jenny and Myron—to our friends, members of our ward, and members of the church. Thank you to the volunteers, to the business owners who donated supplies during the search, and to the search teams for your tireless efforts. A special heartfelt thanks to the members of the Utah real estate and mortgage community, who lightened Ed's burden during the time Elizabeth was missing and helped him to maintain his business at a time when he simply couldn't do it alone. Thank you to the members of the Salt Lake City and other State of Utah law-enforcement agencies, including the Salt Lake City Police Department, the State Crime Lab, the Salt Lake County Sheriff's Department, and the FBI. Thank you to Salt Lake City mayor Rocky Anderson for not giving up hope and keeping the investigation alive. Thank you to the Intrepid Group and to all the members of the media who stood by our side every day and broadcast updates on Elizabeth's story. We would never have been able to bring Elizabeth home without all of you—especially John Walsh, *America's Most Wanted* and *The John Walsh Show,* and the teams at *Good Morning America,* the *Today* show, the *CBS Morning Show, Larry King,* and *48 Hours.* Thanks to all of the print media who never stopped writing about Elizabeth's kidnapping.

We especially want to thank our publisher, who believed that we should write this book the way we wanted to. Thank you to our editor, Trace Murphy, for giving us the freedom to tell our story. Thanks to everyone at Doubleday, including Suzanne Herz for all of your publicity efforts, Joan Schadt, Michelle Rapkin, Michael Palgon, and Steve Rubin. Also, thanks to Adam Mitchell for all of your terrific help in indexing and researching materials.

We want to express our deepest love and appreciation to our six children—Charles, Elizabeth, Edward, Mary Katherine, Andrew, and William. This has been a journey of hope and prayer for all of us. We love you very much. We know these months have not been easy on any of you, but together, with love and commitment, we remain a family.

To our coauthor, Laura Morton. We feel blessed to have found the right person to help us share our journey. Laura shared our vision for this story from the moment we met. We feel that she truly walked in our shoes. She helped us to express ourselves on a subject that was so very hard for us to revisit. Thank you for your sensitivity and support throughout the writing process. We will never forget the tears, joy, and laughter spent on this endeavor. We believe without a doubt that our paths were meant to cross.

And the miracle continues. . . .

Bibliography

Chabot, Sen. Steve (Ohio). "Victims' Rights Amendment Hearing Before the Subcommittee on the Constitution"—May 9, 2002.

Fattah, Ezzat A. "Victims' Rights: Past, Present, and Future."

Jerin, Robert. "A Historical Examination of Victims' Rights in the United States."

Lord, Janice. "National Constitutional Amendment for Victims' Rights"—2002.

Swavy, Joseph. *State News.* "US Legislators Seek to Amend Constitution"—2002.

Contact Information

Laura Recovery Center
307 B-1 South Friendswood Drive
Friendswood, TX 77546
(281) 482-5723 fax: (281) 482-5727
www.LRCF.org

America's Most Wanted
P.O. Box Crime TV
Washington, DC 20016-9126
(800) CRIME-TV

National Center for Missing and Exploited Children
Charles B. Wang International Children's Building
699 Prince Street
Alexandria, VA 22314-3175
Phone: (703) 274-3900
Fax: (703) 274-2200
Hotline: (800) THE-LOST (800-843-5678)

NCMEC/California
18111 Irvine Blvd., Suite C
Tustin, CA 92780-3403
(714) 508-0150 fax: (714) 508-0154

NCMEC/Florida
9176 Alternate A1A, Suite 100
Lake Park, FL 33403-1445
(561) 848-1900 fax: (561) 848-0308

NCMEC/Kansas City
1018 W. 39th Street, Suite B
Kansas City, MO 64111
(816) 756-5422 fax: (816) 756-1804

NCMEC/New York
275 Lake Avenue
Rochester, NY 14608
(585) 242-0900 fax: (585) 242-0717

NCMEC/Manhattan Affiliate
395 Hudson Street, Floor 10
New York, NY 10014
(212) 366-7880 fax: (212) 366-7881

NCMEC/Metropolitan New York
769 Elmont Road
Elmont, NY 11003
(718) 222-5888 fax: (718) 222-5889

NCMEC/Mohawk Valley
247 Elizabeth Street
Utica, NY 13501
(315) 732-7233 fax: (315) 732-2465

NCMEC/South Carolina
2008 Marion Street, Suite C
Columbia, SC 29201-2151
(803) 254-2326 fax: (803) 254-4299